HOW TO PREPARE FOR RETIREMENT

A SIMPLE GUIDE TO ENJOY A SUCCESSFUL RETIREMENT

H. DOMINGUEZ

Copyright © 2018 H. Dominguez
All rights reserved.

No part of this book may be reproduced or transmitted in any form or by any electronic or mechanical means, including information storage and retrieval systems, without written permission from the author, except for the use of brief quotations in a book review.

Published by
Q&A Publishing
25 Old Kings Hwy North # 13-280
Darien, CT 06820-4608

www.moneyconsiderations.com

Cover photo by G. Crescoli.

ISBN 978-1-7329573-3-6

ACKNOWLEDGMENTS

Thanks to my wife for all her help and support.

DISCLAIMER

The content of this book contains personal opinions of the author regarding financial and economic matters. It is for educational purposes only. Neither the author nor the publisher are engaged in rendering professional services including, but not limited to, accounting, tax, legal or investment planning. The information contained in this book is not intended as a substitute for such professional services, and if specific advice is needed or appropriate, the reader should seek out and engage a licensed professional.

The author and publisher expressly disclaim any liability, loss, or risks taken by readers who directly or indirectly act on this information. You are solely responsible for your own decisions and actions, and their results.

The fact that an individual, organization or website is referred to in this work as a citation or a potential source of further information, does not mean that the author or the publisher endorses the information or recommendations they may make. Further, readers should be aware that websites listed in this work may have changed or disappeared between when this work was written and when it is read.

CONTENTS

PART IV
MAKING AND IMPLEMENTING A RETIREMENT PLAN

PREFACE

When most people think about retirement, usually the first thing that comes to their mind is how much money they will need to have a nice retirement. How can you retire if you won't have the resources to pay for all your expenses?

However, once you start thinking about that fundamental question, you realize it is difficult to reach the right answer. Besides, you become aware that the financial aspect of retirement is critical, but is tightly interconnected and influenced by other elements which can play a significant role in how enjoyable your retirement could be.

After doing research, I discovered that making sense of the information available about retirement was going to be difficult. There are different ways to approach retirement. Many aspects must be considered, some are complicated. In fact, entire books focus on just one or a few of those aspects. I was feeling overwhelmed. I only wanted to know what steps I should take to make sure I could enjoy the retirement I wish.

In the end, I thought that an effective way to integrate all the information I had researched would be to write a brief book that could be read in two hours or less, containing all the fundamental aspects anyone must consider to create a simple but reliable and workable plan for his or her retirement. This is that book.

It is structured in four sections. The first addresses how your financial, professional, and personal and family situations have a direct influence on when to retire. The second section analyzes how the answers to three questions can be critical to having a successful and happy retirement. In the third section, the essential financial elements are reviewed. From how to figure out how much money you need to pay for your retirement, what to do if you have not saved enough, and how to invest your retirement savings, to which withdrawal strategy you should follow once retired to guarantee you don't deplete your savings prematurely, and how to handle your taxes during retirement, among others.

Finally, in the fourth section, you will find ideas to improve your retirement, and information about what kind of financial advisors could better help you if you decide that you want help with your retirement planning. Also, the importance of doing a "test-run" of your retirement plan and, how to keep track and monitor its implementation, so you can make timely adjustments that might be required if there are changes in your situation or the economic environment.

To save you time and effort and make it easier and more practical to follow the steps and some methods explained in the book, you can download templates—which you can modify—that help you categorize your expenses, and calculate how much money you will need to pay for your retirement. If you are reading an e-book, you can click directly on links to reach the templates. In the printed version of this book, you will find the URLs you can copy in your browser to get to them.

Additionally, at the end I have included a guide with all the steps mentioned in the book that can help you make your retirement plan, and a list of resources like books, blogs, websites, and online calculators, where you can find more information in case you want to review any retirement aspect in more detail.

PART I

FACTORS INVOLVED IN A SUCCESSFUL RETIREMENT

1

YOUR FINANCIAL SITUATION

While this is not the only aspect to consider when thinking about retirement, it is the one that will determine whether you will be able to retire at all, and what kind of lifestyle you could afford during retirement. As a result, without doubt, it generates more stress than any other among people considering retirement. The reason becomes evident after reviewing some figures.

For example, the Insured Retirement Institute (IRI) has been conducting an annual survey since 2011 when the first baby boomers turned 65, and according to the results of their 2018 survey, only 58% of baby boomers have retirement savings. Among those, 19% have between $100,000 to $250,000 saved, and only 43% have more than $250,000.[1] Other recent studies and surveys found similar results.

Those savings will be insufficient, if we consider that according to figures of the 2017 Consumer Expenditure Survey prepared by the Bureau of Labor Statistics of the Department of Labor, the average annual expenditure of people 65 years and older was $49,542.[2]

That might explain why the 2018 survey of the IRI also found that 69% of Boomers expect Social Security benefits to be a significant source of income for them in retirement.

The list of questions many people have about the financial aspects of retirement is long. Reaching clear and supported answers is not always easy, particularly for those with limited financial knowledge or who don't enjoy delving into financial issues. Questions such as:

- How much money do you need to live a comfortable retirement?
- How does that compare with what you have saved?
- What can you do to close the gap?
- How will your expenses change during retirement?
- In what kind of investments should you keep your savings?
- How much can you spend every year without depleting your savings?
- How can you be sure that your money will last as long as you and your spouse or partner are around?
- Is there a way to guarantee you will be able to pay at least for all your essential expenses in retirement?
- How can you plan to deal with the impact of inflation on your cost of living?

You have probably been asking yourself many of those same questions. Unfortunately, there is not a unique correct answer to them because they involve too many variables and, besides, there's no way to know in advance how they will behave in the future. Variables like the rate of return we can expect to get from our investments, the inflation rate during our retirement years, how long the current tax rates and regulations will remain the same, or what will be our lifespan.

However, as you will see in the chapters in Part III of this book, if you do your homework, it's possible to get useful answers that will allow you to find the best steps to increase your possibilities of reaching a financial position that would make possible the type of retirement you want.

2

YOUR PROFESSIONAL SITUATION

Another essential aspect to consider in your retirement plans is your professional situation.

For people working as employees, studies show that the level of retirement and healthcare benefits offered by the companies they work for can directly influence their decision to retire.

In fact, in companies that continue to offer traditional retirement plans also known as defined benefit plans—in which an employee's pension payments are calculated according to the length of service and the salary they earned at the time of retirement—eligibility to those plans plays a major role in when their employees retire.

However, while 59% of Fortune 500 companies offered such retirement plans in 1998, by 2017 only 16% did, and 51% still employ workers who continue to gain pension benefits.[3]

With the reduction in the number of companies offering defined benefit retirement plans and health care benefits for retirees, now for most people, their eligibility to government programs like

Social Security and Medicare is one of the most critical factors in their decision to retire.

But many other aspects of your professional life can influence your decision to retire, or at least your timing. One very important, for example, is your work environment.

You might want to finish a project you have been working on for some time, or take part in a new one that will give you the opportunity to do some work you enjoy or learn about something new (an industry, sector, technology, or market). Or maybe there will be some restructuring or reorganization coming soon to your company or organization that might leave you in a situation where your compensation could improve and affect your income during retirement.

On the other hand, you might prefer not to stay around, if you are feeling under-appreciated or disengaged at work, don't want to take part in a long-term project you dislike for any reason, or a coming merger or relocation of your employer could negatively affect you.

In any case, as important as all the aspects of your professional situation can be in deciding when to retire, make sure you always consider them together with all the other relevant factors.

3

YOUR PERSONAL AND FAMILY SITUATION

Regarding your personal and family situation, there are many aspects that you also need to consider. Let's talk about some of them.

Your Health

How is your health? While it is hard to find reliable information about how many people retire or need to retire for health reasons, multiple sources put this number around 16%. Being forced into retirement for any cause can put most people on a difficult situation, but when the cause is health problems, it can amplify the negative impact on the quality of their retirement.

Your Spouse or Partner

If you are married–or in a long-term relationship–what is your spouse or partner's situation and her or his goals and plans about retirement? Both of you should plan together your retirement and collaborate in all the steps required to make it work, like saving enough money.

However, it is fundamental you two are also in agreement regarding some of the most important points, like when to retire, where, and what you both expect to do during retirement. These are issues you have to discuss as early as possible because unfortunately for many couples, agreeing on them is not as easy as one would think.

For some people the recent or imminent retirement of their spouses or partners make them consider the convenience of doing the same, to become involved in new activities and spend more time together. But be realistic and ponder how well you and your spouse or partner could adapt to spending all that time together. Some couples who retired at the same time, believe doing it at close but different times would have been a better idea. Think about it.

Your Children

Do you have children? If that's the case, hopefully they are productive, self-sufficient adults that don't need your financial help.

Helping adult children won't affect your retirement if you can afford it, but if you are helping them at the expense of your retirement savings, then you will suffer the adverse effects in retirement.

Your Parents

Maybe you are lucky and still have your parents around. How old are they? How are their health and financial situations? Are they financially independent, or do you need to give them some help?

All these aspects must be considered and will influence your retirement plans.

PART II

KEY QUESTIONS TO ANSWER

4

WHAT DO YOU WANT TO DO DURING RETIREMENT?

For some people, deciding what to do once they retire is not that easy.

While in the beginning not having to worry anymore about any of your old job responsibilities can be very relaxing and liberating, after some time many people miss the structure their job used to give to their days. After a while some are stressed. They feel they are wasting their time and should be doing something "productive" with their abilities and passions.

That's not surprising. For many of us, our identity depends on what we do for a living, and even many of our social connections derive from our work, which also determines the structure of our daily lives.

So, to decide what you want to do during retirement, think on what you spend your free time on. Can you visualize yourself doing some of those activities for long periods of time? Or maybe something very different from what you are doing and that you always wished to do but never had time. Alternatively, you may still enjoy your current profession but would love to apply your knowledge and experience to a cause or project you are passionate about while earning money, or perhaps even just doing it as a volunteer.

Have you discussed it with your spouse or partner? What does he or she would like to do in retirement? Are your plans compatible?

When thinking what you want to do during your retirement, keep in mind that multiple studies have found having a structured life is an essential element in a happy life, and also having a meaningful life lessens the effects of aging and increases longevity.

5

WHERE DO YOU WANT TO SPEND YOUR RETIREMENT?

The answer to this question is fundamental, given the effect it will have not only on how happy you will feel with your retirement but also in the total costs you will face during your life in retirement.

First, you need to decide whether you would like to move, and which would be the implications. If you have been living in the same place (or area) for a long period, this can be important. You need to think about the logistical and financial impact of moving (like having to look for a new place, buying or renting a home there, sell your current house, etc.)

If you live in a high-cost area and you move to a less expensive region, moving might make it a lot easier to cover all your expenses with a smaller retirement portfolio. However, don't neglect to consider also how a relocation would affect the level of contact with family members, and your network of friends and acquaintances.

If you conclude that moving might be a good option for you, there are a few key things you should consider when evaluating different places (including your current location). Those things are:

Cost of Living

This is a fundamental factor. Living in some parts of the country is much more expensive than in others, so how long your savings will last depend on good measure on where you live.

State and Local Taxes

You need to consider taxes on retirement income, property, and purchases, and if there are special tax breaks for seniors.

By choosing the right location based on how different places tax seniors, you can make your retirement savings last longer. While the federal government can tax up to 85% of your Social Security benefits depending on your income, there are 36 states plus Washington, D.C. that don't do it—including nine states with no state income tax.[4]

But to determine the more convenient places you need to evaluate all the state taxes. Some states might not tax your Social Security benefits, but tax distributions from your retirement accounts, have high property or sales taxes or both.

Health Care Services Available

Even if you and your spouse or partner are healthy, odds are you might need more health care services the older you get. Verify those services are available, updated, and of good quality. If unfortunately, any of you has a health issue that requires constant or periodic supervision by certain specialists, this point is vital.

Long-term care

As we will see in the next section, long-term care is one of the most critical expense categories for people retired, but its cost can have huge variations between different cities and regions of the country. For this reason, it needs to be one of the key aspects you include in your evaluation of places to retire.

Airports

If you are looking forward to traveling during your retirement, having at least one good airport close by is very important. Large airports tend to offer flights to more destinations and at better prices.

Economy

The unemployment rate, jobs, and population growth can tell you a lot about the general economic situation of a state, its real estate market, and what you can expect from its tax environment.

Crime

I'm sure you don't want to spend your retirement worrying about your safety and the safety of your property.

Weather

Heating and cooling can be expensive. If you can live in a place that enjoys a mild climate all year long, you will be able to reduce your utility bills. If you have never been in an area, don't assume you know the weather. There can be significant differences in climate even between two regions of the same state.

There are websites where you can find plenty of information about most of the towns and cities in the country. Two good options you might want to check are city-data.com and bestplaces.net. Kiplinger magazine offers a useful "State-by-State Guide to Taxes on Retirees."

Some magazines (like for example Kiplinger, Forbes, U.S. News & World Report, etc.) periodically publish articles about places they deem some of the best options for people to retire. While that information can be useful to reduce your options to two or three you might consider worthy possibilities, because every magazine has its particular biases, you will need to visit those places and see for yourself what they offer, what problems they might present, and what level of connection and comfort you feel in them.

Don't forget to take also into consideration how compatible are those places you are considering for living, with what you and your spouse or partner want to do during your retirement.

6

HOW ARE YOU GOING TO GET HEALTH CARE SERVICES?

Health care is the most important obstacle for many people considering retirement and is an issue that can derail your retirement, given the cost of those services and the financial demands they can put on your retirement portfolio. How are you going to get the health care services you and your spouse or partner will need when you retire?

For many years the cost of health care in the country has been increasing at a much higher pace than the inflation rate, and this trend probably won't change soon. For example, information published by the Federal Reserve on July 2017, shows that during the past 20 years the consumer price index (CPI) has increased at an average annual rate of 2.2%, while the price level of medical care at an average rate of 3.6%. That's almost 64% faster![5]

According to the financial firm Fidelity Investments, a 65-year-old couple reasonably healthy who retired in 2017 would need an estimated $275,000 to cover health care costs during their retirement, considering they have an average life expectancy, and not including what they may have to pay for long-term care.[6]

Since the enactment in 2010 of the Patient Protection and Affordable Care Act (ACA), better known as Obamacare, the laws and regulations surrounding healthcare insurance have been going through a dramatic transformation in recent years making it difficult to plan how to manage your health care expenses.

Nowadays, the rules surrounding healthcare insurance are being re-evaluated and subject to constant change, making it even harder to figure out if what works this year will continue to be applicable the next one.

If You Retire at 65 or Older

Your healthcare will fall under the framework established by Medicare if you retire when you are 65 years or older. Medicare was created in 1965 as part of the Social Security Act and is administered by the Centers for Medicare and Medicaid Services, an agency of the U.S. Department of Health and Human Services.

Medicare comprises four parts, identified as Parts A through D:

- Part A covers hospital expenses, and there's no cost for it.
- Part B covers physician visits, outpatient care, some preventive screening services, clinical laboratory, and diagnostic services among others. Its price varies, and premiums increase based on your income.
- Part C, known as Medicare Advantage, is like a private insurance version that replaces the benefits offered by Parts A, B, and D of the "original" Medicare, while also providing some supplemental benefits like vision and dental for example. There is a wide variety of Medicare Advantage plans and thus in premiums. Know that if you choose this coverage, you still need to pay for Part B premiums.

- Part D provides coverage for prescription drugs, and its cost depends on which medicines you take.

In addition, there is also what is known as Supplement Medicare, which covers some out-of-pocket costs associated with services covered by the original Parts A and B plus some added services, so the cost of this coverage can vary widely.

Most people sign up for Medicare Part A when they turn 65 whether or not they intend to use it right away. If you are still working, it will become secondary to your employer group coverage. You can sign up to Parts B and C, and for Medicare Supplement at age 65 or when you come off your employer group coverage, whichever is later. Be aware however, that you should enroll in Part D within the six-month period surrounding the date when you become eligible. Otherwise, you will pay a late enrollment penalty that is added to the monthly premium you will pay for the rest of your life.

The rules that establish how the different aspects of Medicare work, can be confusing and difficult to understand. Many people don't realize how much Medicare costs. Given its importance, I suggest you invest the time to familiarize yourself as much as possible with its operation and costs. An excellent place to start is reviewing the website: medicare.gov.

If You Retire Before Reaching 65

If you are considering retiring or have to retire before reaching the age of 65, getting health care can be a little more complicated. You will need to assess which could be the best option for you from the following.

COBRA

One of the first options could be to sign up for what is known as COBRA (The Consolidated Omnibus Budget Reconciliation Act) through your employer. This will allow you to stay in your employer's group health plan for up to 18 months after you leave the company. In most cases, this can be a good short-term option that will allow you to keep your same doctors and medical routines, while you explore other possibilities, not only for its limited duration but also because of its high cost.

While using COBRA, you will pay not only the part of the cost of the health plan you used to pay for as an employee but also the part that was being paid by your employer. COBRA even allows your employer to charge you for the administrative cost generated by keeping you in the health plan, so you can end up paying up to 102% of the cost of the plan. Find out how long your coverage can last and its price.

Individual Insurance

If COBRA is not available to you or is not a viable option, then you will need to get insurance individually. To get the best possible price for individual insurance you need to review all the options available. You should generally check first the insurance policies offered through your state's health insurance exchange or on the federal site healthcare.gov, in case there's any chance that your income could qualify you for a subsidy provided by the Affordable Care Act (ACA).

The ACA created a subsidy system for what the government considers low- and middle-income families, based upon their income in relation to the Federal Poverty Level (FPL), setting a cap on the amount of insurance premium they have to pay. You qualify for a subsidy when your income is below 400% of the FPL, which in 2018 is $48,560 for singles, $65,840 for couples, and $100,400 for a family of four.

In the healthcare exchanges the ACA requires the states to maintain, you will find multiple policies provided by different insurance companies grouped in four tiers called: Platinum, Gold, Silver, and Bronze. As you move from the Platinum to the Bronze tier, you will find the policies included in each level have a decreasing premium, but higher deductible and out-of-pocket costs. So, if you are in good health and your medical expenses are low, going with a policy in the Bronze tier could be your best option, while a Silver or Gold policy could be better if your health expenses are higher.

Unfortunately, it is not as easy as just determining what tier could be most convenient for you. If you check the different policies available within the level of your choosing, you will realize that the effective total amount of out-of-pocket costs varies depending on what is counted toward them.

After reviewing the health insurance exchanges, don't forget to check also what policies you can get directly from the insurance companies, through a web broker like ehealthinsurance.com or by working with a health insurance agent (you can look for one in your area at nahu.org). Some insurers offer off-exchange policies with different premiums, cost-sharing arrangements or provider networks than what their on-exchange versions have.

Health Savings Accounts (HSA)

Some insurance plans in the Bronze and Silver tiers are considered High Deductible Plans (their deductibles are a minimum of $1,350 for individual plans or $2,700 for family plans.) The advantage of these plans is that they allow you to contribute to a Health Savings Account.

The funds you contribute to this account are deductible for income tax purposes up to a certain annual limit (up to $6,850 for family coverage or $3,450 for individual coverage—plus an extra $1,000 if you will be 55 or older by the end of 2018.) They grow tax-free, and you can withdraw from them also tax-free, as long as you use them to pay for qualifying medical expenses.

Another aspect to consider is when to buy the insurance. You can buy one that follows the regulations of the ACA, within 60 days of losing your job-based health plan. Otherwise, wait until the next open enrollment period, which goes from November 1st. to December 15. However, remember that since the ACA has been in force, if you don't have health insurance for over two months, you will pay a stiff penalty for every additional month you don't have insurance. This sanction will stop being applied after 2018.

Short-Term Insurance

The Affordable Care Act allowed insurance companies to sell health insurance policies that didn't offer all the coverage required of the regular policies sold within the exchanges, but limited such plans duration to a maximum of 90 days. However, in August 2018, the Trump administration announced new rules that will allow insurers to sell short-term health insurance good for up to 12 months and make those policies renewable for up to three years.

These policies can be a viable option for some people. They offer a more limited coverage (most exclude maternity care, preventive care, mental health services or substance abuse treatment), and can also contain annual and lifetime caps on benefits, or cover fewer prescription drugs. But because of that, their cost is lower than the more comprehensive ACA insurance. Be aware insurers can bar people with pre-existing health conditions from these policies or limit their coverage.

Direct Primary Care

Other option to consider is Direct Primary Care (DPC). Under this model, family physicians offer an alternative to the predominant fee-for-service model. Doctors charge their patients a monthly, quarterly, or annual fee that covers all or most primary care services, including consultative services and the opportunity to get medications and lab tests at or near wholesale prices.

A variation of this same model is what it's known as concierge medicine, which is like a modern version of the relationship that existed between doctors and their patients before the current predominant model of third-party payers and managed care companies emerged.

Given that at some point you probably will need medical services that go beyond primary care, you still should buy a high-deductible policy to cover those instances. It is also important to mention that the IRS doesn't consider the cost of DPC services as eligible to be covered with funds in your HSA.

Faith-Based Health Care

Another alternative, at least for some people, could be the faith-based health care ministries. These work like private insurance where its members, who share similar beliefs, pool resources to pay for their expenses when they have health problems. In these plans, people pay the same and are entitled to equal benefits. There are no government regulations or insurance companies involved.

The Christian Healthcare Ministries (CHM) is a good example of these entities. It is defined as a "nonprofit health cost-sharing ministry," through which Christians share each other's medical bills. CHM offers three main programs that cost $150, $85, and $45 and share 100% of the bills for any medical incident up to $125,000 after members cover the first $500, $1,000, or $5,000 respectively. Members can choose an optional program called "Brother's Keeper" which covers catastrophic medical bills (defined as those exceeding $125,000 per illness.) This program has a variable quarterly fee, plus a $40 nonrefundable fee.

As you can see, the cost of this type of program is substantially lower than health care insurance plans. Another advantage of these plans is that if you are a member, you could be exempt from the ACA penalty for not having insurance, but as I mentioned before, this no longer will be an issue next year. Some other faith-based health care ministries are Altrua HealthShare, Medi-Share, Liberty HealthShare, and Samaritan Health Ministries.

Planning for Long-Term Care

Many people do not include in their retirement planning the high likelihood they might need long-term care, and that can be a big mistake considering how usual and expensive it is.

The information available shows that between 50 and 70% of people over the age of 65 will require long-term care services at some point. This means they will need help with at least two fundamental activities of their daily living such as eating, bathing, or dressing, known as custodial care.

In many cases, someone first receives care at home for several months and later moves to an assisted living facility. Around 60%

of the people who stay in an assisted living facility will later need to move to a nursing home.

According to the Genworth 2017 Cost of Care Survey prepared by Genworth Financial with information from surveys applied to over 15,000 long-term care providers, these were the median annual costs of long-term care:[7]

- Adult Day Care (5 days/week): $18,200
- Assisted Living (one-bedroom): $45,000
- Homemaker Services (44 hrs/week): $47,934
- In-Home Health Aide (44 hrs/week): $49,192
- Nursing Home (semiprivate room): $85,775
- Nursing Home (private room): $97,455

Costs like those can wreak havoc in most budgets. It is crucial to keep in mind that Medicare only covers home care for limited time, after a hospital admission that lasted three days or more, and it doesn't pay for "in-home care" when it is not considered "skilled nursing care" that is "medically necessary." Skilled nursing care is the one provided by credentialed health care providers (or technicians under the direct supervision of credentialed providers) and includes things such as physical or respiratory therapy, wound care or IV medication.

Another vital factor to consider that we had already mentioned, is the enormous variation in health care costs between different places. As an example, the median daily cost for long-term care in a semi-private room in 2016 was $148 in Texas, but $407 in Connecticut.

As you can see, because of the considerable impact the high cost of long-term care can have on your finances, choosing a place where it is a little more reasonably priced or maybe buying insurance, can be extremely important to protect your retirement savings. In Chapter 15 we will discuss what you need to consider when analyzing whether purchasing long-term health care insurance might be a good option for you.

Do Your Best to Stay Healthy

It would be difficult to overemphasize the importance that doing your best to stay healthy can have, not only on your financial situation but also on your general happiness during retirement.

PART III

THE FINANCIAL FACTOR

7

KEY FACTORS YOU WILL NEED TO ESTIMATE TO PLAN FOR RETIREMENT

Do You Have Enough Money to Retire?

Let me start by establishing that it's not possible to determine a specific and definitive answer to the question of how much money you need to pay for your expenses during retirement.

Even if there was only one correct way to calculate how much money you will require during retirement, as I mentioned before, some key factors you would need to take into consideration in that calculation can not be known in advance. Factors like your life expectancy, the general inflation rate, the return you will get on your investments, and how much taxes you will have to pay. Let's talk about those factors.

Life Expectancy

This is a fundamental factor, given that the amount of money you will need during retirement depends on the expected duration of your and your spouse or partner's retirement. Besides, your estimated life expectancy is an important consideration when making other decisions, such as when to take Social Security benefits; deciding if taking a lump sum payment or the annuity payout option in case you are entitled to a pension; and whether to buy an immediate annuity, long-term care insurance, or keep your life insurance.

Based on data compiled by the Social Security Administration (SSA), a man reaching age 65 in May 2018 can expect to live on average until age 84.3, and a woman until age 86.6. However, those are the averages, and around one out of every four 65-year-olds today can expect to live past age 90, and one in ten past age 95. You can use the life expectancy calculator on the SSA website to check your number.

There are several other life expectancy calculators you can use to help you come up with a better and more realistic estimate for you and your spouse or partner. Some of them are:

- The Livingto100 calculator (living100.com), based on data from the New England Centenarian Study, which is the most extensive study in the world of people who lived to 100.
- The Blue Zones Vitality Compass (apps.bluezones.com/en/vitality). This is a calculator developed by a publisher focused on discovering the best strategies for longevity, based on info from those places in the world where people live long lives.
- The LifeSpan Calculator (media.nmfn.com/tnetwork/lifespan) from Northwestern Mutual. It has the additional value of providing information, regarding how your lifestyle choices and health factors can affect your longevity.

Inflation

The rate of inflation is important for two reasons. First, to calculate how much money you will need to cover your expenses during retirement, you need to estimate what could be the average annual rate of inflation for the period between now and when you are planning to retire.

Second, because the impact inflation has on your purchasing power. Trying to increase your income every year just to maintain your purchasing power can be a real challenge for everyone, but even more for a retiree. The average annual inflation rate from 1914 to 2017 was 3.2%, calculated based on the current Consumer Price Index published by the Bureau of Labor Statistics of the Department of Labor.

The average annual inflation during the last fifty years has been a little over 4% (4.12%), because of the unusually high inflation during the 70s and the first half of the 80s. If we consider only the latest 20 years, the average annual inflation was a little over 2% (2.16%).[8]

However, we need to keep in mind that many financial and economic analysts consider that the current rate of inflation is rather an anomaly, produced as a consequence of all the financial measures taken by the Federal Reserve Bank to help the economy recover after the economic crisis of late 2007 and 2008. Those analysts consider that it's probable the distortions in the economy created by the measures implemented by the Federal Reserve during the last ten years, will produce higher rates of inflation in coming years.

We cannot underestimate the adverse effect that inflation has on our purchasing power, even at low rates. For example, an average annual rate of inflation of only 2%, will decrease your purchasing power by 33% in twenty years, and if the inflation rate goes to 3%, then your purchasing power would lose a 45%. At that rate of inflation if in your first year of retirement you need $50,000 to cover living expenses, twenty years later you would need almost $91,000 to pay for the same things!

The impact of inflation has an inverse relation to your income level, so having a higher income will allow you to handle more easily price increases on essential products and services. Also, inflation has a different impact on your finances depending on your retirement phase.

Many financial analysts who work with retirees have observed that most retirees go through three noticeable phases. The first one, which loosely spans from the 60s to early 70s is characterized for higher spending on activities that fill the retirees new free time (travel, golf, new hobbies, etc.) During the second phase, their spending on all those activities tends to decrease. This phase goes from the mid-70s to mid-80s. During the third phase, most of the expenditure on travel and entertainment disappears or is reduced, but is replaced with an increase in spending on health care. These phases can change depending on the general health of the retirees. We have already discussed how the cost of health care has been increasing above the rate of inflation.

As we will see when we talk about where to invest your retirement savings, one critical way to protect yourself against the pernicious effect of inflation is to make sure that a reasonable percentage of your income in retirement comes from investments that keep pace and even grow more than the inflation rate, like stocks for example.

Return on Your Investments

The average annual rate of return for stocks is usually determined by calculating the performance of those that are part of the S&P 500 index. This index was called Composite Index when introduced in 1923 and included just a few stocks. In 1926 it was expanded to include 90 stocks, and in 1957 included 500 stocks. The average annual rate of return of the S&P 500 from 1928 to 2017, including price appreciation and dividends has been 11.53%.

If we consider what has been the performance of bonds, the average annual rate of return of the 3-Month Treasury Bill for the same period from 1928 to 2017 was 3.44%, and for the 10-year Treasury Bond 5.15%. The average of those two is 4.3%.[9]

Based on the rates of return mentioned for stocks and bonds, if your investments were allocated 50% in stocks and the other 50% in bonds, you might expect a return of around 7.9% before taxes, supposing the behavior of the markets doesn't change too much.

These numbers while useful for estimation purposes won't reflect the exact rate of return you will have in your investments. That rate will depend on future economic and financial conditions, the specific allocation of your investment portfolio, and the particular stocks, bonds, or any other investment instruments in it.

Taxes

As you will see in some of the following chapters, you need to take into consideration the impact taxes will have in your retirement income. Always think what income you will get from your retirement portfolio after tax.

Trying to project tax rates two or more decades into the future is difficult. It implies not only estimating the future tax brackets. Increases in income can trigger taxation that goes beyond just the tax bracket itself and could include the impact of deduction thresholds such as those for medical expenses and miscellaneous itemized deductions, the phaseout of itemized deductions and personal exemptions, the effect of Medicare taxes, etc.

Besides, higher income levels can affect how Social Security benefits are taxed and trigger income-related adjustments to Medicare Parts B and D premiums.

Your first instinct might be to calculate the state and federal taxes based on the current tax rates. However, remember the tax cuts consequence of the recently passed Tax Cuts and Jobs Act are temporary and will apply only until December 31, 2025. After that date, unless Congress passes a new law before, the tax rates effective on 2017 will be applicable again in 2026. Considering this, in any calculation you do it might be better to estimate your taxes based on rates that applied in 2017.

8

HOW DO YOU DETERMINE HOW MUCH MONEY YOU NEED TO RETIRE?

The process to determine how much money you will need to cover your expenses—and those of your spouse or partner—during retirement, is not as difficult as some people might think, but there are some things you should be aware of.

If you review some of the books and articles that analyze this issue, you will notice the process they follow to estimate how much money you will need in retirement is very similar. Their main difference is that some start that process with your income, while others prefer to begin with your expenses.

Step 1 - Option A: Beginning with Your Income

Among the reasons given to start the process to estimate how much money you will need in retirement based on your income, is that most people have a much better idea of how much they earn than about their real expenses. In fact, according to a 2018 Consumer Financial Literacy Survey prepared by Harris Poll, only "two in five U.S. Adults (40%) have a budget and keep close track of their spending."[10]

Replace 80% of Your Income

Many financial advisors consider that people will need from 70 to 85% of their income at the time they retire, to keep more or less the same lifestyle during retirement. So, they think for practical purposes you can assume you will cover your expenses during retirement with around 80% of what you will earn just before retiring.

This "rule of thumb" reflects the adjustments in spending that historical statistics show when people retire. The 2017 Consumer Expenditure Survey prepared by the Bureau of Labor Statistics of the Department of Labor every year, shows, for example, that the average expenditures for that year for someone in the age bracket between 55 and 64 years old was $64,972. For someone 65 years or older was only $49,542, which is 23.75% lower.[11] That difference is close to the 80% considered the "rule of thumb."

Following this approach to estimate how much money you will need in retirement based on your income, you need then to multiply your current income by 80%, which is the percentage of your earnings you want to replace in retirement.

Project What Your Annual Income at Retirement Should Be

Once you have done that, you need to project how much that income will be by the time you retire. To make this a little easier use the table below, which shows the factors to apply to the current income, depending on how many years you are away from retirement and the average annual rate of inflation you estimate for that period.

Average Annual Inflation Rate %	Years to Retirement				
	5	10	15	20	25
3.2	0.00	0.00	0.00	0.00	0.00
4	1.17	1.37	1.60	1.88	2.20
4.5	1.22	1.48	1.80	2.19	2.67
5	1.25	1.55	1.94	2.41	3.01
5.5	1.28	1.63	2.08	2.65	3.39
6	1.31	1.71	2.23	2.92	3.81
6.5	1.34	1.79	2.40	3.21	4.29
7	1.37	1.88	2.57	3.52	4.83

Table 1

For example, if the present value of the income you want to replace in retirement is $50,000, you plan to retire in 15 years, and you think the average annual rate of inflation between now and your retirement will be 4.5%, then just multiply 50,000 by a factor of 1.80 based on the chart, so your target annual retirement income will be $90,000.

You will notice that the first average annual inflation rate included in the chart is 3.2%, no 3.0%. This is because as you might remember when we talked about inflation in the previous chapter, that was the average rate from 1914 to 2017, calculated based on the current Consumer Price Index published by the Bureau of Labor Statistics of the Department of Labor.

If you would like to consider a different inflation rate or number of years to retirement than the ones included in *Table 1*, you can calculate the corresponding factor for those values, by adding 1 to your chosen rate of inflation (in decimals) and powering that sum to the number of years until you retire. So, if for example, you are estimating an average annual inflation rate of 4.5% and you plan to retire in 17 years, then the calculation to determine the corresponding factor would be 1.045 (17)—1.045 power 17 equal 2.113.

Be aware that this method of beginning with your income instead of your expenses won't be accurate if there is not a correspondence between your income and your expenses. This will be the case when for example your expenses are higher than your income, because you are using credit to pay for things, or if your costs are much lower than your income because you are saving a good percentage.

Step 1. Option B: Beginning with Your Expenses

The financial advisors who favor starting the process to estimate the money you will require to pay for your retirement based on your estimated expenses during retirement, recognize that this can be more difficult for many people, but argue that the benefit of that little extra effort will be a more realistic estimation.

Besides, even if you are part of the 60% of people not doing it, tracking your expenses once you retire would be useful, helping you to use in the most effective way the income you will have available.

To track your current expenses in a detailed and systematic way, first begin by analyzing your expenses of at least the last 12 months. You can easily do this by reviewing all your bank and credit card statements for that period. If you didn't keep them, remember that almost all financial institutions allow you to download your statements from their websites.

It's essential to gather the information for the previous 12 months, because if you try to do it only for a shorter period like three or six months, you increase the probabilities of leaving out some seasonal expense that fell outside that period, but that could be significant.

You can do all this analysis by using pen and paper, but it would be much more practical and easier to store all this information in a spreadsheet created in your favorite application (MS Excel, Google Sheets, Libre Office, Numbers, etc.)

The best way to go, would be to group your expenses based on broad categories and subcategories, like the ones shown in the next page.

Housing	
	Mortgage or Rent
	Insurance
	Property Taxes
	Maintenance
Food	
	Groceries
	Eating Out
Transportation	
	Cars (Loan or lease payment)
	Insurance
	Taxes
	Gas
	Maintenance
Health Care	
	Insurance
	Out of pocket payments
Personal Care	
Clothing	
Utilities	
	Electricity
	Gas and heating oil
	Phones
	Internet
Entertainment	
	TV (Cable and Streaming Services)
	Books and Magazines
	Movies, theater, shows.
Travel	
	Transportation
	Lodging
	Food
	Other expenses
Taxes	
	Federal
	State
	Local
Gifts and Donations	
Other/Miscellaneous	

Estimate Your Expenses in Retirement

Regardless of how you decide to do it, once you have identified your actual expenses for each category, think how those expenses will change when you retire. Also consider any expenses that will disappear, like those related to your work, such as the cost of commuting, your contributions to Social Security, Medicare, and your retirement plans.

Include any new one-time or repetitive expenses. Are you planning to travel? If you are still paying your mortgage, when will you finish and have those funds available? If you are planning to move, how will your expenses be affected? How much will the relocation process cost?

Don't forget to budget for what you will have to pay for Medicare (check medicare.gov) or private health insurance. Your employer might have been paying all or a good part of your health insurance premiums, and now you need to budget for that expense. What kind of health insurance you plan to have and how much does it cost?

Keep in mind that as we have seen, expenses during early retirement are higher because of the costs generated by traveling, recreation, and hobbies, but people tend to reduce their spending the older they get. According to figures of the 2017 Consumer Expenditure Survey mentioned above, the average annual expenditure of people 75 years and older was $41,849, or 23.91% lower than people in the 65 to 74 years range ($54,997).[12]

This reduction in expenses as we get older is because people spend less in certain categories such as housing (usually no more mortgage), transportation (a reduction from two to one car), food (less "convenience food" and going out), entertainment (less expensive), and consumer goods (by not replacing appliances and furniture if they work, and not buying fancy gadgets).

By the way, don't forget to consider some monthly savings to pay for those items that eventually will need to be repaired or replaced, like your home appliances or your car.

Estimate the Future Value of Your Expenses

Now that you have estimated your expenses once you retire, calculate their future value by the time you retire to compensate for the loss of purchasing power caused by inflation. To do that, multiply the amount of your estimated expenses once you retire by the corresponding factor shown in the Table 1 included before, depending on the years you are away from retirement and the average annual rate of inflation you estimate for that period.

Finally, get into the habit of continuing to track your expenses. While you could do it with a spreadsheet, it would require a good deal of discipline and attention to detail. A better and a lot easier way to do it that would need much less of your time and be less prone to errors would be to use any of the popular personal finance applications like Mint, Quicken, Personal Capital, Moneydance, or Banktivity.

Step 2. Estimate Your Fixed Income in Retirement

Now that you know what income or expenses you will need to cover, your next step should be to estimate the fixed or guaranteed income you expect to have as a retiree.

Fixed or guaranteed income is any income you will receive periodically and for a fixed known amount, like your Social Security benefits, a pension (if you have one), income from an annuity, maybe some royalties, etc. If you own rental properties, you could include the income they produce here, as long as you make reasonable adjustments for those occasions when that income might be interrupted for short periods (between tenants or when they have problems paying the rent). Few people own rental properties (approximately 11%), but this is an investment that, when well-managed, can be a reliable source of income and one that usually keeps pace with inflation.

A) Social Security

While sometimes under-appreciated by some people given all the talk in the media about social security going "broke," for many people Social Security benefits are a vital source of income during retirement. According to the Social Security Administration, in 2018, 48 % of married couples and 69 % of unmarried persons receive 50% or more of their income from Social Security.[13]

Keep in mind that the average monthly payment in 2018 is around $1,404 per month. Those who had the maximum allowable taxable earnings for at least 35 working years and retired at full retirement age receive $2,788. However, because of the way social security benefits are determined, the percentage they represent of your total pre-retirement income moves in inverse proportion to your income. This means that the percentage of your pre-retirement income that your social security benefits will replace, will decrease as your income increases. Someone with an income of $50,000 could replace let's say 35 % of that income with his or her social security benefits, but someone with an income of $200,000 will only be able to replace 16 % of that income.

You qualify to receive a social security retirement benefit, by having at least 40 quarters of work in a job covered by Social Security, and its value depends on your highest 35 years of earnings. You can claim full benefits (known as your primary insurance amount or PIA) once you reach full retirement age, which varies based on when you were born. If you were born between 1943 and 1955 your full retirement age is 66 and increases by two months for every year between 1955 and 1959. For those born in 1960 or later, full retirement age is 67 years old. You can apply as early as when you are 62 years old; however, the amount of your benefits will be reduced 25% from what you would had received at full retirement age.

You can get a good estimate of how much you will receive in retirement benefits, by visiting www.ssa.gov and opening your account to view your personalized Social Security statement, or you can get a gross estimate by providing some basic information about your earnings and retirement age by using the *Social Security Quick Calculator*. Another option is to use the *Social Security Retirement Estimator* which will estimate your benefits based on your actual Social Security earnings record.

If you are married, don't forget to consider also the income your spouse can receive from the Social Security. Remember that when you file for retirement benefits, your spouse may be eligible to receive a spousal benefit, which can be as much as half of the amount of the benefit you receive if you opt to retire at your full retirement age, and depending on your spouse's age at retirement. Your spouse must be at least 62 years old to qualify for the spousal benefit.

In case your spouse is eligible for a retirement benefit based on her or his earnings, your spouse will receive the spousal benefit, only if it is higher than the retirement benefit she or he would qualify for.

Once you know how much it would be your and your spouse's annual Social Security benefit in today's dollars, add them and then project its future value by the time you will retire. To do this, you can use the same table you used before to project the future value of your expenses (Table 1 on page 47).

Your Social Security benefits receive cost-of-living adjustments

(COLA) based on the Consumer Price Index for Urban Wage Earners and Clerical Workers (CPI-W) prepared by the Bureau of Labor Statistics, so I suggest you use the historical rate of inflation of 3.2% included in the table, projected by the number of years until your expected retirement.

B) Pension

Another source of guaranteed income, but one that only a small percentage of people will receive from their employer, is a defined benefit pension plan. According to the Bureau of Labor Statistics of the Department of Labor, from 1980 to 2008 the percentage of people taking part in pension plans fell from 38 to 20%. That percentage has continued to decrease every year, and many experts expect the vast majority of those pensions will eventually be ended.

C) Annuities

An annuity is a contract between you and an insurance company to which you make a single payment or a series of payments, and the insurance company becomes responsible for making a lump sum payment or a series of payments to you, immediately or in an agreed future. Annuity contracts can be complicated, and they are an instrument not well understood by many. Especially by those who put the value of annuities only on their return on investment (ROI), and don't see them also as insurance against living a long life, which can be a serious problem if at some point you no longer have the financial resources to support yourself.

However, there is one type of annuities that can be a handy instrument for retirement planning, and that is the Single Premium Immediate Annuity (SPIA.) In an SPIA you pay to an insurance company or other financial institution a sum of money (known as a premium), and they will pay you a certain amount of money periodically (monthly for example) for the rest of your life. There are fixed annuities that pay a fixed amount every chosen period, and variable annuities which payout is linked to the performance of a mutual fund. Variable annuities are more expensive and complex, so most financial advisors consider fixed annuities a better option.

To calculate your estimated annual guaranteed income, add the expected future value of your total Social Security retirement benefits (if married, including those of your spouse) at the time you will retire, any income you will receive from a pension, from an annuity, and from any other source you might expect any fixed income.

Step 3. How Large Should Your Retirement Portfolio Be?

Now you need to determine if there is a difference and how large it is, between your estimated required annual retirement income (or from your estimated retirement expenses), and your total retirement income represented by the sum of your projected fixed-income at retirement plus the income you can expect to get from your retirement portfolio every year. To do this, subtract from your estimated required annual retirement income or from your estimated retirement expenses (depending on which one you calculated), your projected fixed-income in retirement. The difference is the amount of money you will need to get every year from your retirement portfolio. As an example, if your estimated required annual retirement income or retirement expenses were $59,000 and your projected fixed-income $30,000, then you would need to get $29,000 every year from your retirement savings.

In Chapter 12, we will discuss some of the best strategies to determine how much money to withdraw from your retirement savings to cover your living expenses without depleting those savings, and among those strategies, we will analyze in more detail the so-called "4% Strategy." For the moment, let's say this strategy considers that if you withdraw 4% of your retirement savings plus an annual adjustment to account for inflation, your savings should last at least 30 years if your investments allocation is 50% equities and 50% fixed income.

Following the 4% Strategy, if you multiply by 100 the amount of money you will need to get every year from your retirement portfolio as determined above ($29,000) and then divide the result by 4, you will estimate what should be your ideal retirement portfolio by the time you retire ($725,000).

Step 4. Estimate the Future Value of Your Current Retirement Portfolio

To estimate the future value of your current retirement portfolio, you need first to add the value of all your retirement investments: stocks, bonds, mutual funds, ETFs, money market, REITs (Real Estate Investment Trusts).

Once you have determined the current value of all your financial assets, you need to estimate how much you expect your retirement nest egg will grow from today to when you are planning to retire.

As we saw in the previous chapter, based on the historical average annual rate of return for stocks and bonds from 1928 to 2017, and if we consider an allocation of 50% equities and 50% bonds, we could expect an average annual rate of return of around 7.9% before taxes.

You can estimate the future value of your portfolio by multiplying its current value for the corresponding factor show in the table below.

	Table 2						
Years to Retirement	5	7	10	12	15	20	25
Average Annual & Growth							
3	1.16	1.23	1.34	1.43	1.56	1.81	2.09
5	1.28	1.41	1.63	1.80	2.08	2.65	3.39
7.5	1.44	1.66	2.06	2.38	2.96	4.25	6.10
7.9	1.46	1.70	2.14	2.49	3.13	4.58	6.69

So, if for example the current value of your financial investments is $150,000, you expect to retire in 15 years and get an average annual return of 7.5%, multiply $150,000 by 2.96 to determine the estimated future value of your investments when you retire ($444,000 in this example).

If you want to calculate the factor for a different rate of return or number of years to retirement than the ones included in *Table 2*, you can do it using the same formula as before. Add 1 to your chosen rate of return (in decimals) and power the result to the number of years until you retire. Let's say for example you want to consider an expected average annual return of 6% and that you plan to retire in 9 years, then the calculation to determine your factor would be 1.060 power 9 = 1.689.

Step 5. What's the Gap in Your Retirement Savings?

That gap is the difference between your ideal retirement portfolio ($725,000 in our example on Step 3) and the future value of the one you have ($444,000), which in this example would be $281,000.

It is essential to determine the size of the gap because it will give you a good idea about the magnitude of the measures you will have to take–which we will review in Chapter 10–to reduce that gap as much as possible, or even eliminate it, by the time you retire.

Don't Forget About Taxes

Keep in mind that all the calculations included in the four previous steps don't consider the impact of taxes. Your net income will be less, so you will require a larger retirement portfolio to account for the taxes you will have to pay.

You will have to pay income tax on any money you withdraw from your tax-deferred accounts, probably on at least part of your Social Security benefits, any pension you might receive from your employer, and on part of any payments you might get from some annuities. Portions of your retirement portfolio might be subject to different tax treatments depending on the type of accounts your funds are invested in (your assets location.) For example, money coming from investments in retirement accounts (IRA) or 401(k) accounts will be taxed as income, while funds from ROTH IRA or 401(k) accounts won't be taxed when withdrawn. This is discussed in more detail in Chapter 14.

Note.- In my website *Money Considerations*, there is a spreadsheet with a template to do all the calculations mentioned in this chapter, that you can download and modify for your specific circumstances or needs. You can find it at moneyconsiderations.com/tools/.

9

USING RETIREMENT CALCULATORS

If you don't want to manually do all the calculations required to determine how much money you will need for retirement, you can use one of the multiple retirement calculators available. If you are a "numbers person" or like to tinker with spreadsheets, there are many retirement calculators available, with different levels of accuracy, ease of use, and costs–but most are rather inexpensive.

To provide results as accurate as possible, a retirement calculator should allow you to input all the variations to customize the data to match your current situation. You will need to adjust at least four primary groups of variables:

- **Age:** current age, target retirement age, and life expectancy.
- **Income:** current annual income, and expected income in retirement and sources.
- **Assets:** current accumulated assets, and target assets.
- **Rates:** predicted rates of return on investments, inflation rates, and estimated tax rates.

Other variables that some calculators will allow you to modify are for example those related to lifestyle—like smoking—or health issues that might affect your life expectancy, variations on annual income or expenses, different economic scenarios, and withdrawal strategies.

The more variables you can adjust to your particular situation, the more accurate and relevant the results provided by the calculator can be, but also more complexity is added.

Ease of use is critical to make sure you understand the logic behind how the calculator uses and processes the information you input, and what are the assumptions it is making. You should not use a calculator that is a black box, where you don't understand what calculations it is doing. Also important is how easy you can change inputs and save results, so you can compare how changes in different situations would affect your results.

Because of all the factors already mentioned plus the calculators' inherent limitations, not one will tell you with 100 % precision how much money you will need in retirement. The best strategy is to try two or three calculators and compare their results and understand the different assumptions that might produce variations on the results. The usefulness of retirement calculators will depend on your understanding of all the financial concepts involved in retirement planning, and how each calculator incorporates them in its operation.

Some retirement calculators that offer the possibility to do a decent amount of customization and that you might want to evaluate are:

- NewRetirement (newretirement.com/)
- MaxiFi (maxifiplanner.com/)
- ESPlanner (esplanner.com/)
- Fidelity Retirement Income Planner

(fidelity.com/calculators-tools/planning-guidance-center) —you don't need an account with Fidelity to use this tool.
- OnTrajectory (ontrajectory.com)

All these retirement calculators are web-based, but ESPlanner also has a version that runs on Windows PCs.

If you are interested in testing in more detail the retirement calculators available in the market, one good option is to review the comprehensive analysis that Darrow Kirkpatrick has already done in his blog titled *Can I Retire Yet?*, which I suggest you review because I'm sure you will find other useful information there.

Retire Fit™

Another recently released retirement calculator you might want to check is Retire Fit™ (arnexa.com/retirefit.html), created by a company called Arnexa.

This calculator is a little different from the others for two main reasons. The first is that runs only as an add-on to Google Sheets, so you need to have a Gmail account and download the add-on from the Google Chrome Web Store (it's free). The second reason is that, instead of asking its users to answer some typical forecasting questions (such as, how much they expect to spend every year during retirement or what return they hope to get from their retirement portfolio), it provides suggested answers pulled from the analysis of multiple data sets to help its users to estimate their data more accurately.

So, for example, to calculate your retirement expenses in retirement, the calculator provides information about expenditures and incomes broken down by age (or other demographic attributes) collected from public data sources like the Bureau of Labor Statistics of the Department of Labor.

This approach is called "cohort-guided data entry," and looks to enable users to enter more accurate data. Once you have entered all the information that better describes your situation, the algorithms of the calculator's analysis engine allow you to model different scenarios to consider factors such as asset allocation, fees, and taxes.

Arnexa is working to improve the features of their retirement calculator, by for example, including additional asset classes that can be used within your retirement portfolio information and looking for a way to help users estimate the amount of assets they will have at the start of retirement.

10

HOW TO CLOSE YOUR GAPS

Once you have estimated the expenses and income you expect to have during retirement, it's very likely you will discover there are some gaps between those two.

The Gap between Your Fixed Expenses and Fixed Income

For many people, knowing they will be able to cover all their basic living expenses during retirement, even in a worst-case scenario, is incredibly important for their peace of mind. They want to make sure their fixed income will be enough to pay for those necessary living expenses.

Here the ideal situation would be one in which your sources of fixed income are:

1. Large enough to cover your fixed expenses, and,
2. Able to last at least your lifetime.

However, few people are in that ideal situation. Most people usually have a fixed income gap, and for some, that gap is sizable.

If that's also your situation, one way to cover that gap or at least reduce it could be by investing part of the funds in your retirement accounts or in your other investment accounts in some instrument that could generate the additional fixed income you require.

Among the investment instruments that could be used are CDs, some types of bonds, annuities, etc. Keep in mind, that any of these options imply gaining access to a certain amount of fixed income for the future in exchange for transferring to a financial institution a good amount of money to which you will no longer have access. So, it's important to make sure an investment of this nature wouldn't jeopardize your ability to confront any unexpected expenses. It would be better if you always look to maintain a reasonable amount of liquidity, that would allow you to deal with those situations.

One problem with this strategy is that, even when things are beginning to change, in an economic environment of meager interest rates like the one we have been experiencing during the last ten years, the amount of funds you would have to invest to fill the gap can be rather high.

Let's say for example you have determined that between your fixed monthly expenses and your fixed monthly income there is a difference of $1,500. An option would be to buy a fixed Single Premium Immediate Annuity (SPIA)—see description on Chapter 8.

At the time of writing this, a fixed SPIA has an average monthly payout of $5.30 guaranteed for life (with a minimum payout period of ten years), for each $1,000 invested, for a male age 65 ($5.04 for a female.) This means you would have to invest at least $283,019, which is a substantial amount of money, to buy an annuity that would pay you $1,500 every month for the rest of your life.

This might be doable, depending on how the amount you would have to pay for the annuity ($283,019 in this example) compares to the total value of your retirement portfolio. Moreover, remember you would not only need enough funds to pay for the annuity, but also be able to keep additional funds to pay for the increase in your fixed costs through the years due to inflation, plus your discretionary expenses. Also, please take into consideration the time it would take you to recover your initial investment (more than 15 years in the example of the annuity mentioned before).

To get an idea of how much money you would need to invest in an annuity to produce the amount of income you want, you can check a website like www.immediateannuities.com.

How to Close the Gap Between Your Expected Expenses and Income

Let's talk now, about some of the things you can do to close a gap between the expenses you expect to have in retirement, and the income you could generate every year from your retirement portfolio without depleting it too early.

1. Exchange a Permanent Life Insurance for an Immediate Annuity

When having extra income every month during retirement becomes more important to you than keeping life insurance, this could be an option you might want to explore.

If you have permanent life insurance you have owned for years, talk with your insurance company and other providers, to see if you could convert your insurance to an immediate annuity using what's known as a 1035 exchange (based on the provision of the tax code which allows it.) By doing that conversion, you could buy an immediate annuity which will give you income for the rest of your life (or at least for a guaranteed number of years), without having to take money out from your retirement savings to pay for it. The conversion itself is tax-free.

2. Postpone your Retirement

The first thing most people think when they recognize that their retirement portfolio or nest egg won't be large enough to cover their expenses is to postpone retirement. How good is that option?

On January of 2018, the National Bureau of Economic Research published a paper titled "The Power of Working Longer"[14], in which a group of four researchers analyzed what the best thing you can do to improve your standard of living once retired was. Between trying to increase your savings and postponing retirement, they found the latter is the best option. They discovered that the impact on the retirement income of delaying retirement and applying for Social Security benefits for three to six months was equivalent to saving 1% of your salary every year for 30 years. So, while increasing the amount of income you save is always right, postponing your retirement, if possible, will have a much more significant impact on your financial situation during retirement.

Why is this? For two reasons. The first has to do with the way Social Security benefits are calculated. As I mentioned before, they increase each month that passes from when you reached full retirement age. Because of this, the Social Security benefits for an average worker will rise around 8% for every year he or she postpones retirement. If this person delays retirement for four years, his or her benefits will increase by about 33%. Given that Social Security benefits represent the most important source of income during retirement for most people, increases of those magnitudes can have an enormous effect on their standard of living.

The second reason that makes postponing retirement a more effective option than increasing savings, is that usually by the time you realize the gap between your expected income and expenses in retirement, you don't have too many years to go before you retire, and because of that, you won't enjoy the compounding growth of increased savings.

In addition to higher Social Security benefits, postponing your retirement will give you a little more time to save money, the investments you already have will also enjoy more time to benefit from compounded returns, and on top of all that, you will need to support yourself and your spouse in retirement for fewer years.

3. Reduce Your Current Expenses to Increase Your Savings

If you have not been budgeting, you should do it. Review every one of your expenses, even non-discretionary, and analyze the possibility of decreasing what you are spending.

Most of our spending concentrates on just a few categories. In fact, according to the figures in the 2017 Consumer Expenditure Survey published by the Bureau of Labor Statistics, four categories represented 75% of total household expenses: housing 33.6%, transportation 15.2%, health care 13.4%, and food 12.8%.[15] What this means is that if you want to save a significant amount of money that you could then invest for your retirement, it would be much more productive to focus your efforts on those four categories, rather than just trying to reduce your spending in all the other smaller categories.

The most effective way you can save in those key expense categories is by moving to a place with a lower cost of living. This is an option that at least has to be analyzed if you are serious about saving money. Even if you decide that moving to another town, city, or state would not be workable, don't forget that it could be the only way to extend the life of your retirement investments in a significant way once you retire.

4. Take Advantage of Retirement Accounts

If you have access to an employer-sponsored retirement account —and around 65% of people have— take full advantage, especially if your employer offers to match a percentage of your savings. These accounts are known as 401(k) plans for employees of businesses, 403(b) plans for public education organizations and nonprofits, or 457 plans for government workers.

This is one of the best investments you can make, even if the options offered in your plan are not the best or have high costs. Many employers offer to their employees matching contributions up to a certain percentage of your income. For example, let's say your employer will match $1 for everyone you contribute to your 401(k) account up to 5% of your salary. If your salary is $75,000 and you are saving 10% ($7,500), your employer will then contribute $3,750 to your account. That means you will immediately earn a 50% return on your savings! Where else can you find that kind of return?

There is, however, a limit to how much you can save per year in this type of account. In 2018 you cannot contribute more than $18,500, and to try to help those who are closer to retirement but behind on their savings, the limit for those over 50 years old is $24,500. Your employer contribution doesn't count for these limits, but there is a limit for the combined contributions of $55,000 ($61,000 for those over 50).

If your employer doesn't offer a sponsored savings plan, evaluate the convenience of investing in a traditional individual retirement account (IRA). You can contribute up to $5,500 (or $6,500 if you are over 50), and depending on your adjusted gross earnings, and (when filing jointly) on whether a retirement plan at work covers your spouse, you might deduct all or part of the amount you contribute to the account. Besides, your contributions enjoy tax-deferred growth, meaning you don't have to pay taxes on your investment's gains, and only will pay ordinary income tax when you make withdrawals in retirement.

Another option could be to open a Roth IRA if your income is below the limits set by the IRS ($118,000 for single filers, and $186,000 for married people filing jointly during 2018). The amounts you can contribute every year have the same limits than a regular IRA mentioned above, and while contributions to a Roth IRA are not tax-deductible, they grow tax-free, meaning you will owe no tax when you make withdrawals in retirement, if you are at least 59 1/2 years old and made contributions at least five years prior.

When you reach age 70 1/2, all employer-sponsored retirement accounts are subject to required minimum distributions (RMDs), which are minimum amounts that must be withdrawn every year. One more advantage of a Roth IRA is that there are no required minimum distributions.

5. Health Savings Accounts

Another alternative that can maximize the benefits of any extra savings is a health savings account (HSA).

If you are enrolled in what is called a high-deductible health insurance plan (HDHP), which the IRS defines as one with an out-of-pocket maximum of $6,650 and a minimum deductible of $1,350 for an individual plan or double those amounts for a family plan, you can open an HSA. You can make an annual tax-deductible contribution to an HSA for up to the maximum amount set every year by the government ($3,450 for an individual and $6,900 for a family in 2018, plus a $1,000 catch-up contribution for people 55 or older.) You can invest those funds and will not only grow tax-free, but withdrawals used for qualified medical expenses are not taxed.

6. Keep an Eye on Your Investments' Costs

Sometimes when people realize their retirement savings are not enough to cover their expenses during retirement, they try to compensate by investing their money in a more aggressive way hoping for better returns. Those aggressive strategies usually imply investing in instruments with a high risk of losses and volatility. Keep in mind, that If you don't have other sources of income and need to withdraw money from any of those investments while they are going through a period of low valuation and their price is below your acquisition cost, you lock that loss, damaging your already limited retirement portfolio.

A better strategy would be to focus your efforts on keeping a well-diversified portfolio, composed of low-cost investment instruments like index mutual funds or ETFs. Several studies have shown that over long periods, even minor differences in the expense ratios of funds or ETFs have a significant effect on your results.

Another benefit of investing in low-cost mutual funds or ETFs is that you don't have to spend a good amount of effort and time analyzing individual stocks to form your portfolio.

7. Use the Equity in Your House

Another option to increase your income during retirement could be to use the equity you might have in your house. If you already paid your mortgage or are close to it, evaluate what could be the best option to access that equity.

You would need to consider the following options to determine their feasibility and the benefits they could offer given your situation.

A) Sell Your House and buy another less expensive.

This first option implies that you can find a similar house that works for you, but is cheaper than your current residence. The idea is that then, all the costs associated with home ownership such as property taxes, insurance, maintenance, etc. are also lower, allowing you to reduce the size of your housing expenses, and giving you access to the equity in your previous home.
This can be done by looking for houses in another less expensive part of your town or city, or in another state. If you would prefer to stay where you live, then you might have to explore the option of downsizing.

B) Rent

For this option to work, you should be able to rent a place that works for you and for a lease that would represent meaningful savings compared to your current housing costs. For you to do a proper analysis to see if renting could make sense financially, it is essential to consider all the costs and risks of ownership versus the ones of renting. The New York Times offers a great calculator that allows you to compare all the elements that need to be considered. You can find it at:
nytimes.com/interactive/2014/upshot/buy-rent-calculator.html

C) Get a Reverse Mortgage.

> In a reverse mortgage as its name implies, instead of you making monthly payments to a lender like in a traditional mortgage, the lender makes payments to you, the borrower. The bank or other financial institution, which is the lender, will lend you, but only up to a certain percentage of the equity you have in your house. This because given the way reverse mortgages work, their balances increase over time, so if you were to borrow against all the equity in your house, your loan balance could exceed your home value.

You can receive the money you borrow in a lump sum, through periodic payments (monthly payments for example), by opening a line of credit, or through a combination of some of these options.

The amount you can borrow—known as maximum claim amount or MCA—will depend on your age (older borrowers get more money, and if both spouses are borrowers the age of the youngest one takes preponderance), the amount of equity in your house, and prevailing interest rates (the lower the rates, the more money you can get). The limit for the MCA during 2018 is $679,650.

You don't need to make any periodic payments or leave your house. The balance of this type of loans instead is due once you leave the house, because of death or when you sell the house. However, payment of the loan can become due, if you don't pay the homeowners' insurance, homeowner association fees (if applicable), property taxes on the house, or don't give it basic maintenance.

Most reverse mortgages are paid through the sale of the home, and if the funds from the sale are more than the amount owed, your heirs get the difference. If for any reason—like a fall of the real estate market—the balance of the mortgage was larger than what can be obtained for the house, the difference doesn't have to be paid. However, if your heirs want to keep the house, then the full balance needs to be paid.

To be eligible for a reverse mortgage you must be: at least age 62, have equity in your house (must be your primary residence), and the financial ability to cover its property taxes, maintenance, and insurance.

The cost of a reverse mortgage is not low. There are closing costs similar to those of a traditional mortgage, plus origination fees (up to 2% for a home worth $200,000), an initial mortgage insurance premium (around 2% of the loan amount), and an annual mortgage insurance premium (0.50% of the outstanding mortgage balance.) The interest rates can be fixed or variable, based on an index plus the margin charged by the lender (the index usually is the one-month or one-year London Interbank Offered Rate—LIBOR).

It is important to remember that, once you are aware your retirement savings are running behind of where they should be to provide the income you would like to have during retirement, the sooner you take steps to solve that situation the better your odds will be of finding a solution.

11

HOW TO INVEST YOUR RETIREMENT SAVINGS

To enjoy a comfortable retirement, you need to accomplish four basic things:

1. Save systematically

To accomplish this, you need to make saving part of your budget and consider it another "expense" you need to cover every month, no matter what. This will have the additional benefit of forcing you to keep your expenses under control.

2. Invest Your Savings Successfully

This requires you to choose a strategy to invest your retirement savings in a way that not only protects them against losses, but that at the same time allows them to produce a return above the inflation rate, at reasonable costs, levels of risk, and in a tax-efficient way.

3. Have a reasonable estimate of how much money you need to pay for your retirement (see Chapter 8)

4. Follow an effective withdrawal strategy (see Chapter 12).

An effective strategy will focus on trying to maximize your retirement income while making sure that your savings last as long as you and your spouse or partner.

An investment strategy able to achieve the goals mentioned on point 2, should be structured with the right asset allocation, asset location, and level of diversification.

Let's review those three aspects of an investment strategy.

Assets Allocation

Asset allocation refers to the different asset classes in which you could invest your money, based on the returns you expect will be generated by those assets.

There are four asset classes:

1. Equities (stocks): represent partial ownership of a company.
2. Fixed Income (debt): represents money lent to companies or governments who pay interest. For example, U.S. Treasury, municipal or corporate bonds, certificates of deposit, etc.
3. Cash or Equivalents: like money in savings or money market accounts.
4. Tangibles (real estate, natural resources, and commodities): give you ownership of something physical like land or buildings, gold, oil, grains, etc.

Assets Location

Asset location refers to the type of investment instruments within each asset class in which you are investing and the kind of account where you keep those instruments. For example, do you have the part of your investments allocated to stocks, invested in an index mutual fund or ETF that follows the S&P 500 or in an active mutual fund that invests only in small-cap stocks? In a taxable brokerage account, or in a tax-deferred retirement account like a 401(k) or an IRA? We will talk more about taxes in Chapter 14.

Diversification

Diversification follows the proverbial wisdom of the recommendation not to put all your eggs in the same basket, but it implies much more than just investing your savings in multiple investments. It's a technique that looks to reduce your risk of losing some or even all your original investment and the returns it has generated, by investing in assets that historically have reacted in opposite ways to the same financial and economic situations, meaning they have what's known as a negative correlation.

The most common example of a negative correlation is how the prices of stocks and fixed interest bonds tend to move in opposite directions, given that mostly when investors sell one of these asset classes they invest the proceeds in the other one.

Another factor that can help you diversify investments within the same asset class is geography. Many times (but not always), the economies of different regions and sometimes even of different countries within the same region, behave in very dissimilar or contrasting ways.

To have an adequate level of diversification of your retirement savings is essential you diversify at two levels. First, by investing in different asset classes (for example stocks, bonds, real estate, cash, etc.), and then by acquiring different investments within the same asset category (like for example multiple stocks but in various industries, sectors, and regions; bonds of different types and durations, etc.)

To have a good level of diversification in your retirement portfolio, you don't need to invest in many stocks and bonds. You could invest on just a few mutual funds or ETFs (maybe even only two) that focus on the main asset classes, like for example, in one of those that try to replicate the results of a broad market index like the S&P 500, and in another of those that look to replicate the general performance of the bond market. Here, by investing in just those two mutual funds or ETFs, plus having a reserve of cash, you would have a decent diversification while making it easy to manage and keep track of your investments.

How to Diversify Your Investments Portfolio

To diversify your investments portfolio, you need to know in what asset classes to invest, how much money put in each one, and how to get a reasonable diversification within each of those categories.

To get the best answer to all these questions, you need to consider some factors such as your age, your time frame for investing, your willingness and ability to take a risk (volatility and loss of capital), and the size of your retirement savings.

It is generally accepted that young investors who have a long time to invest, should hold a more substantial portion of their portfolios in high-risk/return assets such as stocks, than those with a shorter time frame. The reasons for this are that people with long time horizons for investing can enjoy the compounding effect of the higher returns offered by more risky assets, while they continue to work and accumulate savings, and can more easily withstand short or mid-term volatility.

Older investors might stop working and accumulating savings in a not too distant future and require using their accumulated savings to cover their expenses in retirement, so they tend to prefer safer, less volatile investments, even if that represents getting lower returns. Besides, as we will see later, suffering losses very close to or early in your retirement, could affect very negatively the amount of income you could withdraw over your lifetime.

The size or amount of your retirement savings plays an essential role in your diversification strategy for very practical reasons. You would need a good number of individual stocks and bonds, on top of a decent amount of cash or equivalents, to create a portfolio with a reasonable level of diversification. To do that requires a rather large capital. On the other hand, you could reach a similar level of diversification if you invest in mutual funds or ETFs (Exchange-traded Funds), and you could do this even with a much smaller capital.

For all these factors, a diversified portfolio can look very different for every investor.

How to Determine the Best Asset Allocation for You?

How do you decide how much money to put in any asset class? Alternatively, expressed on more technical terms, based on what we discussed before, what should be your asset allocation?

As it is often the case nowadays, you can find several asset allocation calculators online. You can check one at this URL: https://www.bankrate.com/calculators/retirement/asset-allocation.aspx

However, if you prefer a more active approach, there are a few strategies you can consider to help you determine an asset allocation that might work best for you. Let's review some of them.

1. Keeping Your Age in Bonds

For a long time, this strategy has been recommended by many financial advisors, not only because of its simplicity but also because it is useful. It means what its name implies. For example, if you are 40 years old, keep 40% of your retirement savings invested in bonds and the rest in stocks. If you are 50 years, then 50% in bonds, and so on.

The effect is that as you get older, your allocation to stocks will decrease and your allocation to assets with less risk will increase. This is known as a declining equity glide path.

However, in response to increases in life expectancy which could cause people following this strategy to invest too conservatively, not growing their retirement portfolio enough to last as long as their lifespan, some financial advisers recommend that instead you subtract your age from 110 or even 120, and use the result to determine what percentage of your portfolio to invest in stocks.

Following this recommendation, it would mean that someone 60 years old should have 60% in stocks and equities (120-60=60) and 40% in bonds.

You need to keep in mind this kind of asset allocation could leave you exposed to a lot of volatility, and you might not be able to handle it. Remember for example 2008 when the S&P 500 fell almost 37%. Could you handle that kind of fall, which would represent a little over one-fifth of the value of your portfolio?

It would be crucial that you have other assets in your portfolio with a negative correlation to stocks, or which value is not affected by market movements (such as cash and equivalents), that you could use to withdraw enough money to cover your expenses until the stock market recovers. Otherwise, you would reduce the life of your portfolio.

2. Investing in Balanced Funds or ETFs

These investment instruments earn their name, by investing in a way that balances their positions in stocks and bonds, keeping a relation between them that can go from 70/30 to 50/50. Some examples are Vanguard Balanced Index Admiral (VBIAX) and Fidelity Balanced (FBALX).

3. Investing in Target-Date Funds

Target-date funds work similarly to balanced funds, but following a formula based on the number of years to the target date. They follow a declining equity glide path, reducing their allocation to equities and becoming more conservative by increasing their allocation to fixed income investments.

Two types of target-date funds can be identified depending on what kind of glide path they have. The first type is made up by the so-called "To" funds, which are those that adjust their asset allocations every year up to their target year and then stop. This group is the most conservative, and usually by the time they get to the target year they hold from 30 to 40% of their assets in stocks.

The second type follows a glide path that takes them "through" their target date, and then continue to adjust their asset allocation. These funds typically have 50% of their assets mix in stocks, but by the time they reach the end of their glide path that percentage has been reduced to 30%. The duration of the post-target-date glide differs depending on the investment company offering the funds and goes from 7 to 19 years. At the end of the post-target-date glide period, the funds tend to merge with some of their retirement or income funds, and from that point, their stocks-bonds allocation remains unchanged.

Because of all this, it's important if you are considering investing your savings on target-date funds, that you understand their objectives regarding asset mix, glide path and its duration, costs, and options at the end of the glide path.

Investing in balanced funds or ETFs or target-date funds can be an easy, practical, efficient, and effective way to invest their retirement savings. Not only you can get a good level of diversification, but you will also avoid having to concern yourself with periodically rebalancing your investments. Besides, you can find some funds that have not only good records but also very reasonable costs.

4. Based on Your Ability to Handle Losses

In this strategy, first, you need to determine what level of losses you would tolerate without losing your cool and selling. One problem is that if you have not been investing in the market long enough to have already suffered the effects of a significant bear market, this strategy might not be the best for you.

Most people's opinion about the amount of losses they can take before feeling the need to run for the exit and leave the stock market, changes after they have experienced firsthand a substantial correction in the market or a full-blown bear market.

To better decide the amount of losses you could take, it might be a good idea to think about those losses not only as a percentage of your portfolio but also in absolute dollar terms, particularly if your nest egg is not too small. This is important because you will not react the same way to a paper loss of $5,000 than to another of $50,000, even if both represent a fall of 20% of your portfolio.

Once you have decided how many losses you think you can take, to determine what should be your allocation to bonds, subtract from 100 double the percentage drop of your total portfolio that you decided you could tolerate. So, if for example, the maximum percentage loss you think you could handle is 20%, then your bond allocation should be 60% (100 - 20 x 2)

5. Based on Your Capacity to Handle Losses

The previous strategy is based on your subjective opinion of the amount of losses in your investments you can take, without panicking and selling them, making then those losses effective and permanent.

This strategy is based on more objective elements, such as the time it usually takes the market to recover from a bear market and the amount of money you need to cover your annual expenses.

Historically, the market has taken from three to ten years to recover from a bear market, depending on its magnitude. As you may know, a bear market is commonly defined as the one in which investment prices drop more than 20% from their most recent high. A bear market happens on average every 3.5 years—more often than many people think. From 1900 to 2014 there were 32 bear markets. Among the worst are the one in the 1930s when the market dropped 83.4% over a little more than 33 months, the one in the 1970s when the market fell 48% during 19 months, and more recently in 2007-2009, when the market dropped 57% over 17 months.

According to financial analyst and journalist Mark Hulbert, it takes the stock market an average of 3.2 years from the beginning of a bear market to go back to where it stood at before (considering dividends and inflation).[16]

Based on this information and considering how much money you need to cover your annual expenses (on top of your Social Security benefits and any pension or annuity you could have), plus the size of your retirement portfolio, you could make the following analysis.

If you need for example $3,000 per month to cover your monthly expenses ($36,000 per year), and you would like to have enough resources at hand to avoid selling any equity at a loss, keep in cash and equivalents plus bonds at least 3 years of expenses ($108,000) or, if possible, depending on the size of your nest egg, a little more. The rest of your retirement savings could be invested then in equities. Or let's say you would like to keep enough funds to cover your expenses during eight years, and you have $500,000 on retirement savings, then you would invest $288,000 in cash (or equivalents) and bonds (57.6%), and $212,000 in equities (42.4%).

Keep in mind that while this type of asset allocation could give you enough peace of mind to make you feel able to navigate through most challenging market periods, the trade-off would be that the level of exposure you would have to equities, might not be enough to compensate for losing purchasing power during your retirement due to inflation. A large allocation to cash and equivalents would drag down the total return of your portfolio.

6. According to the Buckets Strategy

The idea behind this strategy is to determine the allocation of your retirement portfolio, in a way that reduces the possibility of having to sell its assets at a loss but allowing your portfolio to grow enough to keep pace with inflation.

The fundamental idea behind this strategy is to balance the market risk of having a large percentage of your retirement portfolio invested in stocks, with the chance that if you invest in less risky assets your portfolio's growth might not keep pace with inflation, negatively affecting your spending, plus increasing the risk you might outlive your portfolio.

It works like this. Usually, you divide your retirement portfolio into three buckets—but as you will see later, there can be variations that involve a larger number of buckets.

In the first bucket, you keep cash or liquid instruments like CDs, savings, or money market accounts. In the second bucket you invest in high-quality bonds (for example in low-expense mutual funds or ETFs with short and intermediate-term, or municipal bonds). Finally, in the third bucket you invest your money basically in stocks and similar assets with higher-risk of volatility and loss of capital, but also higher potential returns like REITS, high-yielding corporate bonds, and emerging and international stocks (also using low-expense mutual funds or ETFs).

6a. How Much Money to Put in Every Bucket

Regarding how much of your retirement portfolio you should put in every bucket, there is not a unique or correct way of doing it. Financial advisers have different opinions. There is however some consensus that, in the first bucket you should have enough money to cover at least two years of expenses, in the second bucket the funds required during the next three to nine years, and the rest of your money–enough to cover at least ten years of expenses–in the third bucket.

Other advisers think it's better to have three or up to four years of expenses in your first bucket in cash and equivalents, and then divide the rest or your money in two more buckets, 60/40 or 50/50 between bonds and stocks.

6b. Some Variations of the Buckets Strategy

There are other variations of how to set up a bucket strategy. Let's see some of them.

1. Based on the Phases of Your Retirement.
Here you structure the three different buckets according to the funds you will need to cover your expenses as you age. The first bucket will keep enough funds to cover your first five years of retirement, in cash or cash equivalents. A second bucket will contain the funds you will need from your sixth to your fifteenth year of retirement invested in lower risk instruments (no stocks). Finally, a third bucket will have the funds you will need in the long term, invested in equities, giving you the opportunity to grow your money while riding out periods of volatility.

2. Based on Your Needs and Wants.
In this version, your first bucket would have the money you would need to cover all your essential expenses in retirement, invested in a conservative way. A second bucket would have the funds you could use to pay for things that would be nice to have–but not necessities–invested in instruments with moderate risk. The third bucket would contain money for things you might want (splurges or luxuries), invested in riskier, more aggressive financial instruments.

3. Based on Your Spending Categories.
This is a variation of the version mentioned before. In this one, you create multiple buckets (not just three), each

with the funds you will need to cover a specific type of expenses, like day-to-day necessities, healthcare, entertainment, emergencies, luxuries, etc.
This kind of variation of the traditional bucket strategy would be difficult to set up, expensive, and hard to maintain and manage.

7. According to the Level3 Strategy

Another strategy to allocate your investment portfolio is suggested by the founder and chairman of the American Association of Individual Investors, James Cloonan, in his book *Investing at Level3*. Cloonan says most investors have come to equate volatility with risk when the real danger is the chance of investment loss. That when we need to withdraw assets from our portfolio, those assets could have a lower value than what we expected based on our investment strategy.

He advises putting four years' worth of your expenses into cash and equivalents, and investing the rest of your money in equities, without regard to short-term volatility, but instead looking for the maximum return over the long term.

8. Following the 7Twelve™ System

This system tells you how to build a portfolio invested in seven investment categories, utilizing 12 low-cost mutual funds or ETFs. It also guides you to manage the portfolio during your entire lifecycle.

It was developed by Craig Israelsen, who after extensive analysis and posterior back testing, determined that the best level of diversification to provide a good level of capital preservation and growth is reached when you invest your retirement savings in a portfolio with 65% invested in stocks and 35% in fixed income.

The part in stocks should be divided between U.S. Stocks, foreign stocks, stocks of companies that invest in real estate, and in companies investing in natural resources and commodities. To have not only depth of diversification but also deepness, the part invested in U.S. Stocks should be divided between large-cap, mid-cap, and small companies. The part invested in foreign stocks also split equally between those of companies in developed countries and those in emerging markets.

The part invested in fixed income should be divided between U.S. Bonds, non-U.S. Bonds, and cash. Finally, the part corresponding to U.S. Bonds divided between U.S. Aggregate bonds and inflation-protected bonds.

Another benefit of building your retirement portfolio following this structure is that it has a higher probability of lasting at least 25 years. In fact, Israelsen found that if you run 25-year rolling periods from 1970 to 1985 (that is 1970-1994, 1971-1995, etc.), even considering an aggressive initial withdrawal of 10% of the initial value of your portfolio and an annual adjustment for inflation of 3%, your portfolio would survive on average 24.8 years. If instead of using the multi-asset portfolio described above, you had 100% invested in stocks, the portfolio would have an average life of 20.8 years, investing 100% in bonds it would last 17.5 years, and in a mix of 60% stocks and 40% bonds 20.9 years.

As successful as this strategy to build your retirement portfolio can be, don't forget that it will require more effort on your part to set up and rebalance it through the years, than some of the other more straightforward strategies reviewed before.

Connection Between Risk and Return.

You need to always keep in mind, that a fundamental idea in finance is the connection between risk and return. This is why an investment considered almost risk-free like a U.S. Treasury bond, offers a lower rate of return than a corporate bond provided by a company with a much higher likelihood of having financial problems or even go bankrupt than the U.S. Government. Investors have to be compensated for taking on additional risk.

Therefore, even when we can reduce the level of volatility of our investments and try to protect them from devastating losses through diversification, because of the relationship between risk and reward in investments, that same diversification will also reduce the rate of return we can expect.

Importance of Investing in Stocks

In an economic environment like the one we have been experiencing for some years now, where interest rates on saving accounts, certificates of deposit (CDs) and money market are so low, their yield is negative in real terms (after discounting inflation) unless you lock your money for five or more years to get a higher rate. Some bonds can offer you better returns, but investing in stocks is the best way to deal with the adverse effect of inflation.

As we already mentioned in Chapter 7, there is a considerable difference between the average returns you can expect from stocks and bonds. During the last 30 years (1988-2017), the average annual rate of return for the S&P 500 (including price appreciation and dividends) was 12.03%, while for the 3-month Treasury Bill was 3.09%, and for the 10-year Treasury Bond was 6.81%.[17]

While it's true what the legal disclaimers on investment brochures always say about the past performance not being a guarantee of future results, these numbers show the importance of trying to keep at least part of your retirement investments invested in stocks. Not only to compensate for the effect of inflation in your purchasing power but also to allow your retirement portfolio to grow, reducing the probability it's prematurely depleted.

The Sequence of Returns Risk

During your working years when you save and invest that money, your retirement portfolio goes through its accumulation stage. Later, when you retire and withdraw funds from your portfolio to cover your expenses, it will enter its distribution stage.

The so-called sequence of returns risk refers to the possibility of having a series of years with negative returns in your investments, but particularly during the first ten years of your retirement. This could cause your portfolio to deplete much sooner than expected if because of the asset allocation of your portfolio, to withdraw funds you are forced to sell investments below the price you paid for them (their acquisition cost).

Since 1928, the S&P 500 has had two or more years with a negative return on four occasions (from 1929 to 1932, 1939 to 1941, 1973 and 1974, and from 2000 to 2002), and we cannot know when, but the market will go through those periods again. Some of the investment strategies mentioned before, are or can be structured in such a way they help to minimize the negative impact to the life of your retirement portfolio caused by that kind of unfavorable market conditions.

As mentioned before, simple diversification through an allocation on stocks and fixed income assets can in principle reduce your risk of losses. However, despite the ordinarily negative correlation between those two asset classes, this has not always been the case. There have been a few instances when both assets classes suffered negative returns. For example, both the S&P 500 and 10-year Treasury bonds had negative returns during the years of 1931, 1941, and 1969.

The best way to reduce or eliminate the sequence of returns risk, independently of the underlying asset allocation strategy you choose, is to keep a reasonable part of your retirement portfolio in cash and equivalents. That way, rather than having to sell some of your equities or fixed income investments (or both) when their value is down instead of waiting and allowing them to recover, you can withdraw funds from your cash allocation. Later, when those investments not only regained their original value but even generated some gains, you can use them to replenish the part of the cash allocation you used to cover your withdrawals while the financial markets were down.

Finally, it's imperative that once you decide which is the best investment strategy, you follow it systematically, monitoring its performance along the way. Avoid second-guessing the strategy or questioning its effectiveness when the markets have one bad year. If the fundamental elements you took into consideration to choose that investment strategy have not changed, you should not change your strategy. If you are not consistent and change strategies, the long-term returns of your retirement portfolio will suffer, and you might even put the sustainability of your portfolio at risk.

12

DECIDING ON YOUR WITHDRAWAL STRATEGY

Deciding what strategy to follow to determine how much money to withdraw every year from your retirement portfolio is difficult, because it forces you to take into consideration and reconcile two different perspectives.

On the one hand, you want to make sure the amount of money you withdraw every year doesn't risk depleting your retirement portfolio too soon. On the other, you expect the amount you can withdraw every year will be enough to cover all your annual expenses, and that it won't change much from one year to the next one, allowing you to plan and giving you visibility over your financial situation for at least a few years.

Determining Your Starting Point

Whether you decide how much to withdraw based on a dollar amount or a percentage of your portfolio's value, you will always have to determine what will be that initial number.

The Percentage Strategy

If you approach this from the perspective of trying to guarantee the long-term sustainability of your retirement portfolio, your first tendency will be to determine the initial amount to withdraw based on the life expectancies for you and your spouse. So, you may decide your retirement portfolio has to last at least 25 or 30 years, and as a result you will withdraw 4% or 3.3% of its total value the first year (1 divided by 25 or 30), and then determine the percentage to withdraw for successive years by adjusting (decreasing) the number of years you estimate are left on your lifespans.

The problem if you do that, is that you would ignore the impact of the variations on the value of your portfolio every year due to the condition of the financial markets, and the effect of inflation on your purchasing power during retirement. You might risk depleting your portfolio too soon if you underestimate your lifespans. Besides, planning would be difficult, because the amount of your yearly withdrawal could vary substantially from one year to the next one.

The 4 % Withdrawal Strategy

This has become a rule of thumb for many retirees and originated in 1994 when a financial planner called William P. Bengen published an article on the Journal of Financial Planning.

In that article, Bengen after analyzing the historical performance of the markets and inflation since 1926, says that with a portfolio invested 50/50 between U.S. large-company stocks and U.S. intermediate-term government bonds, retirees can withdraw 4 % the first year of retirement, and then adjust that dollar amount to account for inflation every year thereafter and expect their portfolio to last at least for 30 years.

Later, Bengen determined that by introducing some diversification by having a portfolio with an allocation of 35% large-cap stocks, 20% small-cap stocks and 45% intermediate-term bonds, the withdrawal rate can be increased to 4.5%.

This strategy, despite–or maybe because of–its popularity has been the object of some criticism. Some people think the conditions that made Mr. Bengen conclude that a 4 or 4.5% % withdrawal rate was safe were very different to those existing nowadays, where we have overpriced stocks and low interest rates.

Another problem some people see with this strategy is that it is indifferent to the behavior of the capital markets, by increasing the amount the retirees withdraw based on inflation, regardless of whether their portfolio's market returns are positive or negative. Critics say if the market has negative results, but the amounts withdrawn are not adjusted, the retirement portfolio could be prematurely depleted. Likewise, if the market has an extraordinary performance, the retirees could miss an opportunity to increase their spending.

Bengen, who has himself retired, has addressed some of this criticism and said in interviews that it might not be a bad idea to keep 10 or 15% of your portfolio in cash (taking that money from the funds allocated to bonds), just in case you run into a bad or bear market. That way you could live off your cash allocation for some time, and not have to sell any of your stock investments during a bad market environment reducing the sequence of returns risk.

The 4 % rule can be a good starting point, that should be adjusted depending on your situation (health condition, amount of savings, etc.), and the predominant financial and economic climate.

Withdrawals Following a (Traditional) Buckets Strategy

To withdraw the money you need to cover your expenses every year when you are following a buckets strategy (explained in the previous chapter), whether you follow the 4% strategy or any other, the best way is to observe the behavior of the markets.

When the market is having a good year and your stocks are doing well, withdraw your money from your stocks (third bucket). If your bonds are the ones doing better, then take your money from the bonds (second bucket).

When the market is going through a hard period, take out your money from your cash bucket (first bucket). In the case of a prolonged difficult period in the market, you can take the money for your yearly expenses from your bonds if your cash bucket has been depleted. Later, when the market conditions improve, you will replenish your cash bucket by trimming your top performers in your other two buckets.

An advantage of this strategy is that eliminates or at least reduces the sequence of returns risk. Even in the event of an underperforming or even a bear market, you can keep your calm knowing that you don't need to sell your stocks and bond holdings for some years–for how long it will depend on your bucket's distribution–giving them time to recover. This is great considering that since 1926, the most extended bear market lasted 2.8 years, and in average bear markets have lasted 1.4 years.

Let's suppose for example, that you retire having a $750,000 portfolio invested in stocks and bonds and withdraw 4 % during your first year of retirement ($30,000). That year the market goes down 25 %, and by the time you need to withdraw more funds to cover expenses for the following year, your portfolio has now a value of $562,500. If you sell stock or bonds at a loss to withdraw the money you require to cover your expenses, you will reduce the number of shares you own and that would have been available to recover by enjoying any future positive returns.

If the negative returns continue in the market for one or two more years, and you need to sell more stock or bonds at a loss, the damage to your nest egg will increase, reducing the total amount of money you could withdraw over your lifetime.

The Investment Earnings Withdrawal Strategy

In this strategy, you withdraw just the income generated by dividends, interest payments and fund distributions preserving the underlying number of shares of the portfolio.

The first challenge this strategy presents is that your portfolio might not be large enough to produce the amount of income you need or would like, especially in recent years when the Standard & Poor's 500 Index (S&P 500) has been providing a dividend yield of around 2%. Besides, it is likely that this strategy could cause variations in the amount of income you have available every year, making it difficult to plan and budget. Additionally, the amount of income produced by your portfolio may not keep up with the pace of inflation.

These last two reasons will force people trying to follow this strategy, to reach into the capital invested to cover their yearly expenses.

The Feel Free Withdrawal Strategy

This strategy is called "feel free" because it refers to the idea that people who spend at this level should have little to worry about depleting their retirement savings. However, like in the previous strategy mentioned above, having enough money to pay for your retirement expenses is another matter On the other hand, it could impose unnecessary restrictions on the spending of people with considerable retirement portfolios.

This recent and simple method was developed by Evan Inglis, a senior vice president for Nuveen Asset Management. The formula consists on dividing your age by 20 to determine how much can you withdraw every year from your portfolio. So, for example, someone age 65 can spend (withdraw) 3.25 % of his or her retirement portfolio, and someone age 70 can spend 3.5 %.

The Dynamic Spending Strategy

This strategy has been proposed by the Vanguard Investment Strategy Group and is a hybrid between two of the most popular, the percentage of a portfolio and the initial dollar plus inflation strategies. It allows the retirees' annual spending to fluctuate depending on the performance of the markets, while reducing the level of those fluctuations from year to year, by establishing a ceiling and a floor to each year's spending amount.

You determine your annual ceiling based on the percentage you would like to increase your withdrawal from one year to the next if the markets had a positive return the previous year. Your floor is determined by the percentage you're willing (and able) to reduce your spending when the markets had a negative return the past year.

To implement this dynamic strategy, first you determine your yearly withdrawal by applying your chosen percentage to your prior year-end's portfolio balance. Then, you calculate from the amount you withdrew last year, the ceiling and floor you decided. Now you need to compare both numbers.

If the amount to withdraw that you calculated based on your chosen percentage is higher than the ceiling, then you withdraw only the ceiling amount. If it's lower than the calculated floor, then you withdraw the floor amount. You will withdraw the amount calculated based on your chosen percentage when that amount falls between the floor and the ceiling points.

The idea behind this strategy is to keep the retiree's spending consistent but linked to the financial markets' performance to guarantee the sustainability of the retirement portfolio.

Let's see an example of how this strategy would be put in place, based on this information:

- Starting balance: $750,000
- Year 1 portfolio growth: 12%
- Withdrawal rate: 4%
- Ceiling percentage: 7%
- Floor percentage: 3.5%

Year 1

Annual withdrawal amount = $30,000
Starting balance ($750,000) by withdrawal rate (4.0%).
Ending balance = $810,000
Starting balance ($750,000) plus investment earnings ($90,000), minus the annual withdrawal amount ($30,000).
This example assumes end-of-year spending.

Year 2

Initial annual spending amount = $32,400
Starting balance ($810,000) by the withdrawal rate (4.0%).
Ceiling amount = $32,100

Year 1 annual spending amount ($30,000) by the ceiling percentage (7.0%), plus year 1 annual spending amount.

Floor amount = $28,950.

Year 1 annual spending amount ($30,000) minus floor percentage (3.5%), by year 1 spending amount ($30,000).

Determine the spending amount by comparing your results.

Your initial annual spending amount ($32,400) exceeds your ceiling amount ($32,100), so you would withdraw your ceiling amount ($32,100).

13

REQUIRED MINIMUM DISTRIBUTIONS (RMDS)

A different issue, but very related to the strategy to determine how much money to withdraw every year from your retirement portfolio to cover your yearly expenses, is the Required Minimum Distributions (RMDs).

No matter what withdrawal strategy you use, once you reach age 70 1/2, the Internal Revenue Service requires you to make withdrawals from your traditional individual retirement accounts (IRAs, 401(k)s, 403(b)s, IRAs, SEP IRAs, and similar tax-deferred retirement accounts). Roth 401(k) accounts are also subject to required minimum distributions, however they can be rolled into a Roth IRA account, which is the notable exception not subject to RMDs during the owner's lifetime.

To calculate the RMDs for each of your retirement accounts, you divide their end-balance on the prior December 31 by the life expectancy factor corresponding to your age, that the IRS publishes in tables in **Publication 590-B Distribution from Individual Retirement Arrangements (IRAs).**

Keep in mind, that even when the financial company who is the custodian or the retirement plan administrator of the IRA may calculate the RMDs, for the IRS the owner of the IRA or retirement plan account is responsible for calculating the amount of the RMD.

It is important that you plan for any distributions that will be required in the coming year. You will not only need to determine the correct amount to take from your accounts, but know the tax consequences of such distributions, decide what are you going to do with the money, and make sure you take the distributions before the deadline.

While you must take your first required minimum contribution beginning on the year you turn age 70 1/2, that first withdrawal can be made until April 1st of the following year. However, it's important to remember that for subsequent years you must take the RMDs by December 31 of the year, including the second year you will take your RMDs, even if you withdrew by April 1st of that year RMDs corresponding to the previous year.

It is critical you take your RMDs before the deadline, because whatever amount you were supposed to withdraw but you didn't, will be taxed by the IRS at 50%.

Regarding the tax consequences of the RMDs, remember that distributions from traditional IRAs will be included in your gross income and taxed as ordinary income.

Over time the RMDs increase your adjusted gross income and could cause negative effects like reduced tax deductions and can cause you to pay additional taxes such as the Medicare premium surtax, the alternative minimum tax, or force you to include all or part of your Social Security benefits in your gross income, among others.

There are multiple strategies you can explore to determine the best way to manage your RMDs, so plan with enough anticipation.

Depending on your personal and financial circumstances, you could use your RMD to cover your living expenses, reinvest them in a taxable account, donate them to some of your favorite charities (if possible, as a qualified charitable distribution (QCD), which is not included in your gross income but counts as part of your RMD for the year), save them in a short term CD or money market to become part of your emergency fund, or spend them.

You can find detailed instructions about how to handle your RMDs in the Publication 590-B issued every year by the IRS.

14

TAXES DURING RETIREMENT AND HOW TO MINIMIZE THEIR IMPACT

When dealing with retirement issues like: what kind of account you should use to invest your retirement savings; in which type of investment instruments to invest; or, how and how much money to withdraw once you retire, you will have to analyze what would be each of their tax effects, to make sure you will keep as much of your savings as possible.

Using Your Asset Location to Minimize Your Taxes

Reducing the amount of taxes you need to pay, can have a significant impact on the amount of money you will have available to cover all your expenses. One way to do that is by paying attention and being careful with your asset's location.

Most people understand that their assets allocation (what assets to own and in what proportions, as discussed in Chapter 11), is the single most influential decision they can make to influence their portfolio's performance, but many don't know the concept of asset location so well.

Asset location plays a crucial part in a tax-minimization strategy, in which investors place or locate their investments across different saving vehicles looking to generate the highest after-tax return for their entire portfolio.

Optimizing your asset location is important because while you can't control market returns or the tax law, you can control how you use accounts or investment instruments that offer certain tax advantages to increase your net returns. It would help if you familiarize yourself with how the income generated by different saving accounts or investment instruments is taxed, to determine the best asset location to minimize the taxes you must pay.

However, remember that you should always concentrate first on your asset allocation, and only after that, look for the best location for those assets.

Different Types of Investment Income, Different Taxation

As you know, there are multiple sources of investment income recognized by the tax code, which are taxed at different rates. Let's review them.

> **Interests-** Most interest income is taxed as ordinary income, within seven tax brackets that go from 10 to 37% (based on the tax law effective on 2018).
>
> **Capital Gains** - For tax purposes, it is considered that a capital gain is realized when someone sells or exchanges an investment for a higher price than what that person paid for it (his or her cost basis). Here the tax rate to pay will depend on how long the investor held the investment. If the gain was made from an investment held for less than a year, it will be considered a short-term capital gain and taxed as ordinary income. Long-term gains (from investments held for over one year) are taxed under the

new 2018 tax law– and through 2025–at three different rates depending on your overall income: 0%, 15% or 20%. However, because of the additional 3.8% surtax levied by the so-called "Affordable Care Act," capital gains for single filers with net investment income and modified adjusted gross income above $200,000—and married couples filing jointly with income above $250,000—will pay rates of 18.8% and 23.8%.

Dividends - Here the tax code talks of two types. Regular dividends, that are taxed as ordinary income; and Qualified dividends, taxed at the capital gains rates. Qualified dividends are those paid by a U.S. corporation or a qualified foreign corporation, for a stock you owned for over 60 days during the 121-day period that begins 60 days before the ex-dividend date (which is the date by which you must be a shareholder.) The 3.8% surtax mentioned before also applies.

Tax-Advantaged Accounts

The tax code also gives a tax-advantaged treatment to some accounts and investment instruments.

Tax-Deferred Accounts - Money invested in employer-sponsored investment plans like a 401(k), 457 or 403(b) grows tax-deferred, and taxes are only paid when the investor withdraws money from those accounts. Other investment instruments that are also tax-deferred are ordinary IRA accounts, annuities, and the cash surrender value of a whole life insurance policy.

Tax-Exempt Accounts - They are funded with after-tax dollars, and some retirement accounts such as the Roth

401(k), Roth 403(b) and Roth IRA accounts enjoy tax-exempt status. This means their income and earnings are free from taxation, as long as withdrawals are taken at least five years after the contributions to the accounts were made, and if the account owner is older than 59 1/2 years.

529 College Savings Plans - They are also tax-exempt when the contributions are made with after-tax dollars, and the earnings used for educational purposes.

U.S. Savings Bonds - Owners of U.S. savings bonds may pay the taxes yearly as interest accrues or can wait to pay taxes until they cash in the bond, the bond matures, or they transfer the bond to another owner. Most investors defer paying the taxes until they redeem the bond.

The interest income you receive from some securities is exempt from federal or state taxes (or both).

- **Municipal Bonds** - Interest is free from federal income taxes, and in most states, the one you receive from securities issued by municipalities within the state is also exempt from state and local taxes.

- **Bonds issued by U.S. territories and possessions** - Interests are exempt from federal, state, and local income taxes in all 50 states.

- **Treasury bills, notes and bonds** - Interests are subject to federal income tax but are exempt from all state and local income taxes.

- **U.S. savings bonds** - Interest is taxed at the federal level, but not at the state or local level.

When you are evaluating two similar investments, like bonds, but one of them is taxable while the other offers a tax advantage (like a municipal bond for example), you need to adjust the yield provided by the taxable investment to make it comparable to the tax-advantaged option.

Let's say the taxable bond has a yield of 4% while a municipal bond yields 3%. To make the taxable bond yield comparable with the municipal bond, multiply its yield by one minus your marginal tax rate. So, supposing your marginal tax rate is 28%, then you would have: 4% x (1-0.28) = 2.88%. Now you know that in this case, the municipal bond would offer you a better after-tax return.

Portfolio Turnover and Taxes

Besides considering your assets location, another aspect you also need to analyze because of the impact it can have on how much taxes you will pay when investing on mutual funds or ETFs, is their portfolio turnover.

When a mutual fund (or ETF) sells some of its holdings, capital gains that are realized are passed to its shareholders, which triggers a tax liability for shares held in a taxable account. Portfolio turnover is the frequency of changes in an investment portfolio. It is expressed as a percentage and measured by taking the value of securities purchased (or sold, whichever is lower) in the past 12 months and dividing it by the total asset value.

This is a factor that can affect the after-tax or net-return of your investments, and you should consider it at two different levels. First, in any of the mutual funds and ETFs that are part of your investment portfolio, and second, at the level of your investment portfolio.

Actively managed investment vehicles—like mutual funds and now even some ETFs—in which their managers buy and sell positions in different investment instruments trying to optimize their results based on the investment objectives of the fund or ETF, obviously will have higher turnover than passive ones such as index mutual funds and ETFs, that have a high number of transactions only when the indexes they follow suffer any change, which is unusual.

Nevertheless, keep in mind that some actively managed funds make part of their objective to minimize taxes by strategically harvesting losses.

It is also important to mention that, mutual funds and ETFs with high turnover ratios, not only tend to have higher expense ratios, but also transactions costs (which are not reflected in the expense ratio), all of which will negatively affect your returns.

Tax-Efficient Withdrawal Strategies

To minimize the amount of taxes you must pay, you not only have to be careful in what type of accounts and investment instruments you put your savings, but later you need to be cautious with the way you withdraw funds from those accounts and investment instruments during retirement.

To make a tax-efficient withdrawal of funds from your retirement portfolio, you will need to coordinate how much to take from your taxable accounts (which will be taxed at the capital gains rate) and how much from your retirement accounts (that will be taxed as ordinary income).

Many financial advisors think retirees should try to withdraw money first from their taxable investments to allow their tax-deferred retirement accounts to take advantage of the compounding.

One problem with this strategy is that if you need to make a rather large withdrawal (maybe because of an emergency), you risk moving up into a higher income tax bracket.

Other advisors consider a better strategy would be to withdraw the money to fund your spending from your taxable accounts, while also doing partial Roth conversions of your IRA, so that you can fill tax brackets in the early years of your retirement. Filling your tax brackets means that the additional income generated by the partial conversion of your IRA will fill, but not make you exceed the upper limit of your tax bracket. This way, in later years you could withdraw part from your traditional IRA and part from Roth accounts to avoid being placed into higher tax brackets.

Tax Treatment of Your Social Security Benefits

Your Social Security benefits are not exempt from taxes unless they represent your only income, which is not good.

The IRS uses a measure called "provisional income" to determine how much taxes you should pay. You calculate your provisional income, by adding your gross income (pension payouts and retirement-account withdrawals), any tax-free interest, and 50% of your Social Security benefits. If the total is less than $25,000 if you're single or $32,000 if you're married, all your benefits are tax-free. When it falls between $32,000 and $44,000 for married couples ($25,000 and $34,000 for singles), you pay taxes on 50% of your benefits. If your provisional income goes above the top of those ranges, 85% of your benefits will be taxed. To compute your exact taxable benefits, you should refer to **IRS Publication 915.**

Going back again to the importance of where do you live during retirement, you need to consider how states tax Social Security benefits. Thirty-six states plus Washington, D.C. exempt benefits from taxes–or don't have an income tax. The other thirteen follow the same taxation rules as the federal government, but nine offer deductions or exemptions based on your age or income, so you won't have to pay tax on their full amount.

Only in four states (Minnesota, North Dakota, Vermont or West Virginia), 85% of your benefits will be taxed.

Filing Your Taxes

One thing that probably won't get any easier for you once you retire, is filing your taxes. Once you retire, you will probably have a lower income than the one you had during your working years. While that could imply having to pay less in taxes, it is also likely you will have multiple sources of income, which complicates things. You can receive your Social Security benefits, income from your tax-advantaged retirement accounts, maybe also from other investment accounts, a pension, annuities, freelance or part-time work, etc. As you have seen, different sources of income come with their own set of tax rules.

Most people are or were employees, and they have been used to having a single source of income. You receive your paycheck with some withholdings by your employer, who then makes quarterly tax payments to the IRS. In retirement, you will be required to make those estimated quarterly payments yourself.

For paying estimated quarterly taxes, these are the four periods in which every year is divided and their corresponding deadlines:

- January 1 to March 31 deadline is April 15.
- April 1 to May 31; June 15.

- June 1 to August 31; September 15.
- September 1 to December 31; January 15 of following year.

I would recommend you put these dates in your calendar at the beginning of every year.

To determine your estimated tax, it might be useful to use as a starting point your income, deductions, and credits for the previous year (use your federal tax return.) Use **Form 1040-ES** which is a worksheet published by the IRS to provide guidance.

The IRS could impose you a penalty if your estimated quarterly payments are not paid on time, or you don't pay enough estimated tax for the year. One way to avoid this is by paying the same amount of taxes you paid last year, or at least 90% of what you will owe this year, whichever is smaller. However, if your income is more than $150,000 per year, then you are required to pay 110% of what you paid last year.

If you stay organized and keep track throughout the year of your income and expenses and stay informed of changes to the tax laws that could affect you, preparing your taxes for filing should be relatively simple. If your finances are not complicated, it could be a good idea to use tax preparation software like TurboTax or H&R Block for example. However, if your finances are more complex, it might be better to hire the services of a tax professional.

15

PLANNING FOR THE UNEXPECTED

Doing a proper work planning for your retirement implies not only planning how to handle all the expected events but to also be prepared to the best of your possibilities, to manage those unexpected events that could derail your retirement.

Non-planned Early Retirement

Studies by multiple financial institutions through interviews with retirees have found that a high percentage of them had to stop working unexpectedly for different reasons, such as the loss of their job, health problems, or the need to take care of a spouse or dependent.

When people have to retire earlier than expected, they face several challenges. The unplanned loss of income will impact their retirement savings, can force them to apply for Social Security benefits earlier reducing the amount of benefits they will receive, and to handle having a longer retirement period. It's also important to remember, that you cannot access Medicare until you are 65 years old or collect reduced Social Security benefits before you are 62, so if you were to lose your employment before those thresholds, you would have to cover all your expenses from your savings, including the cost of healthcare.

All this underscores the importance of saving early, and as much as possible, because the more money you have saved, the better prepared you would be to handle an unexpected early retirement. But there are other steps you can take.

Having the Right Insurance

One of them is to get the right insurance policies that can protect you against some of those unexpected events that can disrupt your retirement plans.

But even if you could insure against any risk you might face during retirement, probably it wouldn't be a good idea, nor cost-effective. It's better to use insurance only to protect yourself against those risks that could be catastrophic. Among those, I would consider three:

1. Your early death; which most times could have a very negative impact in your spouse's own retirement;
2. Becoming disabled; and,
3. Losing your home or most of your assets.

To be covered against other lesser risks, you could self-insure by creating a good size emergency fund.

Now let's analyze some of the insurance that might help you be better prepared to confront those risks.

Whole Life Insurance - Term Life Insurance

Having a term-insurance policy that covers you during those years when your children depend on the income you are generating then and until just before you retire, might be a good idea. That way if you were to die, at least your family wouldn't suffer the financial impact of your loss.

But if instead of buying term-insurance you bought a permanent policy, probably by the time your children have grown, you will have paid the mortgage on your house (or almost), and saved enough for retirement so you might not need that policy anymore. Don't just stop paying for it and let it end. Keep it to help improve the financial situation of your spouse once you die, if your retirement portfolio is not as large as it should.

Also check if options like surrendering the policy for its cash value or going for what is known as a "reduced paid-up" (where you stop making premium payments but still maintain coverage but with a reduced benefit), might be available to you. Keep in mind the first of these options could be useful, even when you have to pay taxes on the amount that its value exceeds the premiums you have paid.

You may have other options. If you have a permanent life insurance policy, the best idea might be to hire an independent fee-only insurance adviser for help deciding what to do. The fees for such advisor will be low (less than $250 very probably) and well worthy.

Long-Term Disability Insurance

If you are planning to continue working ten or more years because you are depending on those future earnings to secure your retirement, it might be worth considering getting disability coverage. The closer you get to retirement the higher your earnings are, but the likelihood that you might become disabled also increases the older you get.

Your first step should be to check if your employer has coverage available under a group policy, given that it would be cheaper than to get an individual policy. If you need to buy your own individual policy, one way to reduce its cost is to extend what it is known as the "waiting period," which is the time between when you suffer the disability and when the benefits of your policy kick in. The typical waiting period is 90 days, but you could extend it to six months or even a year. To decide the right term, consider the size of your emergency fund.

A disability policy will replace around 60% of your gross salary—but if you lower that percentage, you might get additional savings. This percentage however can be lower for people with high income, given that long-term disability policies usually include a monthly cap to the benefits that they will pay, and in many cases only consider your salary via income and not through bonus or commissions.

Property and Casualty Insurance

Make sure you have enough coverage to rebuild your home, with comparable materials and at current labor costs, in the event of a total loss. Shop around periodically, because the difference in premiums for homeowner's insurance among insurers has been increasing in the last few years (also for auto insurance).

Despite the total liability coverage that you may have by your homeowner and auto policies, I would suggest considering also having an umbrella policy, which provides you extra liability insurance that could even cover you for an amount equivalent to your entire net worth, and it is inexpensive–close to $200 per year for up to $1 million of coverage.

Long-Term Care Insurance

In Chapter 6 we discussed how statistics show that many people will require long-term care at some point in their lives, and how expensive it can be (up to $100,000 or more per year depending on where you live). So, getting coverage against the risk of having to pay for long-term care seems like something worth considering, if you are not rich or poor.

The history of long-term care insurance has not been a happy one. When these policies first caught during the 1980s and 90s, they were based on unrealistic estimates by the insurance companies. They underestimated how much and how fast the cost of long-term care would increase, how many claims would be filed, for how long people would draw payments before dying, and how many people would keep their policies active. They also thought that most people would prefer to stay in their homes instead of moving into an assisted-living facility or nursing home. All this, plus the economic conditions after the financial crisis of 2008 characterized by low-interest rates, contributed to reduced earnings on the customer premiums invested until they were needed to pay claims.

As a result, many insurance companies disappeared. Around a dozen insurers sell the coverage nowadays, down from over 100 thirty years ago. Those that still do, have been forced to increase the premiums charged to their customers in the last few years, sometimes up to 50%, 90% or even more. Despite all this, around a fifth of the U.S. population 65 years old or older (over 7 million people) owns a long-term care policy.

One benefit of all the pricing problems insurers have had is that new policies have been adjusted to offer much more realistic benefits and premiums. Also, the state governments insurance departments who have to approve any increase to premiums, have also learned from all the past problems and seem to be questioning more the insurers' assumptions. Even when all this doesn't eliminate the possibility that you might be hit with a premium increase, the likelihood of a significant increase or multiple increases is much lower today.

This insurance is not cheap. According to the American Association for Long-Term Care Insurance, a trade group for insurance agents, at the beginning of 2018 a policy for a 60-year-old couple that would start with a maximum payout of $164,050 per person and grow 3% per year to $333,000 when the couple is 85, had a cost of around $3,500 in combined annual premiums. However, consider the impact that not having this coverage could have on the quality of your life. Knowing you might have to pay for long-term care with your own retirement funds, could make you limit your spending on some things or activities.

To reduce the cost of this insurance, consider the convenience of extending what is known as the "elimination period," which is the number of days between when you become eligible for benefits and the time the insurer will pay for them. Most policies include a 90-day elimination period. The longer this period, the lower your premium will be. Also, the sooner you buy, the less you will pay. The premiums climb with each year you age.

It's always a good idea to review all your insurance coverages at least every other year, but once you are approaching retirement, a coverage check-up is essential.

Documents You Need in Addition to the Right Insurance

Having life, long-term disability, and long-term care insurance policies will help you and your spouse and family deal with the impact your finances would suffer, if you were to fall ill or have an accident and become at least partially incapacitated. However, there are other aspects you should also consider if something like that were to happen:

1. Who would manage your finances?
2. Who can decide about your medical care while you cannot do it yourself?
3. If you pass away, how can you make sure your assets pass to the people or entities you want?

To guarantee someone you trust can make those decisions on your behalf, in case you became temporarily or permanently disabled to make financial or medical decisions, you need to prepare the following documents:

Durable Power of Attorney (sometimes also referred to as Financial Power of Attorney).
This document goes into effect the moment you become unable to make your own decisions and can give your spouse (or partner) the authority to manage each other's finances, in case any of you become incapacitated.
You can order one very inexpensively from an online legal site (like for example legalzoom.com) but is a better idea to have a lawyer prepare it, even when a little more expensive so that it conforms to your state's laws and it's properly executed. Another advantage of having a lawyer prepare it is that if someone were to challenge the authority of any of the spouses, the lawyer could testify that both were legally able when they signed the power.

It's important to know that some banks and other financial institutions use their own forms, and honor powers of attorney only when certain conditions are met.

Power of Attorney for Healthcare (sometimes also referred to as Health Care Proxy).
This document allows your spouse or any other person you trust, to communicate with the people taking medical care of you, and make any health care decisions for you—including those that might prolong your life.
You can find information about how to prepare this document in the website of the American Bar Association, and a basic form valid in all states except in New Hampshire, Ohio, Texas, or Wisconsin, which have particular requirements.

Living Will (also known as Advance Directive).
This document allows you to provide instructions regarding end-of-life care. It gives you the opportunity to express what kind of medical treatments you would (or would not) want if you became unable to communicate your wishes while suffering a terminal illness. You can find the advance directive form for your state at caringinfo.org

Designate Beneficiaries

To make sure your assets go to the person, persons or entities you want once you pass away, you should start by designating the beneficiary or beneficiaries for every financial account and pension you have. Usually, every financial institution requires that you fill out and sign its specific forms to designate beneficiaries.

Always address who will be your primary and your contingent beneficiary or beneficiaries. A primary beneficiary is someone who gets the money if you die, and a contingent beneficiary, someone who receives the funds in your accounts if you and your primary beneficiary or beneficiaries are dead. Don't forget to designate beneficiaries for all your accounts.

Next, you will have to focus on having the estate planning documents that will designate who you want to receive your personal and real estate property, and if applicable, your business once you die, and do it in the most timely and cost-effective way possible. If you don't do this, then your assets will have to be distributed according to the probate laws of your state, which can establish something very different to what you had wanted.

You will need to prepare a will or a living trust. If you leave a will, all your assets named in it will go through your state's probate process and then be distributed to your heirs. The probate process is different in every state. Its duration can go from around nine months to up to two years or longer and involves executor fees and court costs. If you own property in more than one state, your heir(s) will have to go through multiple probates, each with its own rules.

To prepare a living trust is more expensive than a will, but it can offer advantages. For example, avoiding having to go through probate, make it possible to consider all your property together because it is valid on all states, and staying in effect even after you die, because your assets can remain in your trust and be managed by a trustee you selected, until a beneficiary or beneficiaries reach a certain age. Only then they would inherit following your instructions.

As you can see, estate planning is complicated. You should talk about it with an experienced attorney specialized in this area, that could advise you about the best options, based on your personal situation and what you would like to do with your assets.

Keep all the documents mentioned above together, safe, and in a place accessible by your spouse, or the person you decide in case of an emergency.

PART IV

MAKING AND IMPLEMENTING A RETIREMENT PLAN

16

DO IT YOURSELF OR HIRE HELP?

If you have the inclination, a reasonable level of financial knowledge, and are willing to invest the time, probably you could not only manage your retirement planning and finances by yourself but enjoy doing it. First, during all those years when your primary focus is to choose and implement an investment strategy that will allow you to increase the size of your retirement nest egg. Later, maybe with a little more effort, from the point in time when you create and follow an actual retirement plan.

At the end of this book, you will find a guide you can follow, to make sure you go through all the aspects you need to consider when developing your retirement plan.

If you don't think you have the characteristics that would allow you to manage your retirement planning and finances, or you don't want or don't have the time to do it yourself, then you should look for someone who can help you.

Whom to Hire?

In most cases, that person should be a certified financial planner (CFP), someone who has prepared and passed exams on financial planning. Among the CFPs, I suggest you look for a fee-only CFP, who will charge you by the hour or a flat rate for his or her advice and specific services, and doesn't sell any kind of financial products. You must execute yourself any steps required to implement the information they provide you.

Now, if you would prefer that they manage your investments for you, some CFPs can do it, generally for an annual fee based on the amount of your portfolio (around 1%).

In the Resources section at the end of the book, you will find the name and web links to three networks of fee-only financial planners. Through their websites, you can get information about financial planners in your area.

As we already discussed, not even the best CFP will give you an exact and definitive answer regarding how much money you will need in retirement. However, once familiarized with your current situation and your goals and expectations, a CFP should be able to advise you on fundamental aspects of your retirement plan such as:

- When to apply for Social Security benefits;
- The best allocation and location for your retirement portfolio assets;
- How much income could you expect;
- What would be the best withdrawal strategy to guarantee that your portfolio lasts as long as required; and,
- How to minimize your taxes.

If you hire the services of a Certified Financial Planner, it might be a good idea to look for one who also has among his or her credentials some of the following designations: Certified Retirement Counselor (CRC), Retirement Income Certified Professional (RICP), or Retirement Management Analyst (RMA). To earn these designations, financial planners need to go through a more rigorous preparation.

Keep in mind that good advisors won't make any recommendations to you until they know what's your current financial and personal situation, and understand your goals and expectations for retirement.

17

THREE RECOMMENDATIONS TO IMPROVE YOUR RETIREMENT

There are a few simple principles, that if you keep them in mind and do your best to follow them in anything related to planning your retirement and managing your retirement portfolio, you will not only be much more effective but will save yourself a lot of trouble.

Simplify

Life sometimes can be complicated (OK, many times), so try not to contribute to that by making things related to your retirement more cumbersome than they need to be. Mostly when there are multiple ways to accomplish something, the more straightforward and more accessible option will be the best. More complex and challenging alternatives will be only marginally more effective, making them not worthy of the additional stress they cause.

Following this principle for example regarding how you invest your retirement savings, look to merge your accounts, so that if possible, you don't have to deal with more than two or three financial institutions at the most.

In the same way, try to limit the number of accounts you have of the same type. Some people, for example, have multiple checking accounts (do you really need more than two?), credit cards, and accounts with three or more brokerages (again, why do you need more than two?). They keep open the 401(k) accounts they have had with every past employer, instead of doing a rollover and merging them in the one with the financial institution that offers the best investment options and costs.

This principle also applies to your investments. As we have seen, you don't need to have many mutual funds or ETFs to get a decent level of diversification that can give you reasonable protection against loses and a good return on your investments.

The same goes for your withdrawal strategy. Use one that increases the likelihood your retirement portfolio will grow and last enough to cover all the expenses during your, and your spouse's retirement. One that is also easy to follow and manage, especially as you get older.

It's always a good idea to look for the most effective but straightforward way to manage all your financial matters.

Prevent

You have seen how by their very nature, some factors that have an enormous impact in your retirement cannot be known with certainty in advance: the rate of inflation, return on investments or taxes, and obviously, our own longevity. This makes our planning efforts more difficult, but you can reduce the risk of getting into real trouble, by at least not making overly optimistic assumptions about those factors, considering their history and any known elements that can influence their future situation.

When planning, try to determine at least two scenarios, considering not only the most probable situation for those factors, but also the worst, and look in advance for a "Plan B" for those cases, or at least give some thought to what possible adjustments you would have to do in such scenarios.

Prevention can also have a significant impact on your health. Obviously, there will always be those diseases that can hit you no matter what you do. However, according to many studies, most senior citizens suffer one or even two chronic illnesses that probably could have been avoided with simple lifestyle changes, like maintaining a healthy diet and following an exercise routine.

Considering the cost of healthcare and the demands it can impose on your retirement savings, anything you can do to try to prevent health issues is probably the best investment you can do toward a happy retirement.

Don't Forget Taxes

As you saw in Chapter 14, given the impact taxes can have in your net income, carefully analyzing every financial decision related to your retirement to try to reduce that impact as much as possible, is well worth the effort and time required. Decisions like the type of investment instruments in which you invest your money, the kind of accounts you use, and your withdrawal strategy can produce very different tax results that you should consider.

18

DOING A TRIAL RUN

Unless you work for an organization or company that allows you to take a sabbatical or anything similar, or you own a business and could take time off for a more extended period than usual, doing a "trial run" of your retirement might not be possible for most people. This shouldn't be an excuse to not try, at least for short periods, some of the most crucial aspects of your retirement plan, to check the soundness of your assumptions and see if some adjustments may be in order.

Planning to Move?

If you are planning to move once you retire, you don't want to realize after six months in a new town, city or state, that you made a mistake and is not what you had expected, or a place where you cannot envision yourself spending the rest of your retirement.

So, it's vital that you do a careful analysis to identify the right place for you to retire. To do that, you need to plan with enough anticipation. You could investigate options through the internet and magazines, to determine which places seem to better cover the requirements you look for.

Once you have found a few options, it might be a good idea to use vacation time to visit them, so you can compare the information you have gathered about the place with reality and see how you feel there. Is it what you were expecting? How are the people? What's the vibe of the area? Do you like it?

During these exploratory trips, it's essential to keep your eyes and ears open. It wouldn't be unusual that while visiting one place you learn about another one close by, that was not even in your radar, but that might be a better option. Try to relax and disconnect from your daily routine and the stress of your job on these trips, but keep in mind the primary goal of evaluating the place you are visiting as one where you would enjoy retiring to.

Check the availability and quality of all those places important for someone living there, like supermarkets, cleaners, shopping centers or malls, restaurants, movie theaters, concert halls, museums, hospitals, etc. How about the cost of living? Do the prices you see correspond with what you were expecting?

It's also a good idea to read any local newspapers or magazines. They can give you a good idea of what are the most important and pressing issues in that place. Try also to find out if there are any local communities in social media you could keep an eye on.

Once you have decided which is the place where you would like to spend your retirement years, is essential to make multiple visits and stay for periods as long as possible. Try to stay at a place in the area of the town where you would like to live to get a better feeling of the zone. Check also the availability of homes for rent or sale within your budget and see if they would work for you.

One final suggestion. If you are considering moving just to be closer to your children and grandchildren, think carefully about it. If you have two or more children and they live in the same place, then it might make sense.

However, planning to move to the place where your only child lives (or the only one with children), might not be the best idea. Even when he or she might not have any plans to move in the foreseeable future, there is no guarantee your child's situation won't change and have to move somewhere else.

In such a case (which happens more often than some people think), what would you do? Move again? Can your retirement savings absorb the impact of the costs involved without affecting your financial situation, particularly if you bought a house? And, if something similar happens again?

Testing Your Budget

Another aspect of your retirement plan you should validate is your budget. This is better done as you approach your tentative retirement date, but not as close to it that you won't have the time for another trial if you need to adjust your plans.

Try to live on the budget you have set for yourself and your spouse/partner after you retire. Make adjustments for those expenses that cannot be reduced until you retire, but see how realistic are the costs you budgeted for all the other categories included in your retirement budget. Also, make sure you left no expenses out of your budget.

How well could you live within the retirement budget? If after the trial period you decide the budget you set is not realistic, then you must determine what steps to take. If you decide you need to increase the amount to cover your yearly expenses, will you need to save a little more money to grow your retirement portfolio by the time you retire? Will you have to postpone your retirement for a little while? Maybe both?

In case none of those adjustments seem to be enough to make your numbers work, then you will have to consider all the options to reduce your expenses, from downsizing (some people prefer to call it "rightsizing"), to moving to a place with a much lower cost of living.

Testing What You Plan to Do in Retirement

During a retirement trial run, also try to check if the activities you expected to be doing in retirement really would work for you. As I mentioned before, many studies have shown that retirees feel better about their lives when their days are structured and have routines. This seems to be especially crucial for people who used to be involved in high-pressure jobs before retiring.

How does it feel to do all the activities you planned to do? Are they keeping you busy enough but without stressing you out? Or maybe you think that after a while you might find them a little boring? Are you getting the level of social interaction you want? Would you like to do any changes to your original plan?

Remember that a trial-run will not only allow you to test several aspects of your retirement plan but also give you the opportunity to re-evaluate your retirement goals.

19

TRACKING THE PERFORMANCE OF YOUR RETIREMENT PLAN

Monitor and Adjust Your Retirement Plan

You need to review periodically (every quarter or at least twice a year), if your retirement is going according to your plan, and if not, make adjustments before things get out of control and radical measures are required to correct the course.

Probably the best way to monitor your expenses, income, and the performance of your retirement portfolio, is to use the right personal financial tool. Some tools make it possible to keep an eye in all those aspects with little effort and in a short time (check the ones mentioned in Chapter 8 for example).

In addition, you will also need to evaluate your retirement plan and make any necessary adjustments, every time any aspect of your health, finances or lifestyle suffer an essential change.

Also, in case drastic changes affect any or some of the key financial aspects on which you based your retirement plan (like taxes, interest rates, inflation, etc.), then you might need to adjust your plan. Hopefully, that won't be necessary.

Review the Performance of the Key Factors

What should you check to see if your retirement is going according to your plan? You need to review if the key factors that made your retirement plan workable have behaved within the parameters you had estimated. Here I'm talking about the following factors.

- What was the return of your retirement portfolio last year?
- What was the inflation rate for the same period?
- Were your expenses in line with the amounts estimated in your budget?
- Did you withdraw the amount of money calculated in your retirement plan?

You need to specify the cause or causes of any significant variation (more than 5%), and try to understand if they were a one-time event or might represent the beginning of a change in the trend they were following. You might need to wait until you have the results of at least two years to answer that.

Once you are sure there has been a change in the trend followed by one factor, then you need to decide if the new trend makes any change or adjustments necessary to your retirement plan to ensure its long-term effectiveness.

If you are using a retirement calculator, the process to review the performance of your plan should be simple and show you which are those aspects of your plan that need any adjustment.

Warning Indicators

Two things might indicate there is something wrong with your plan, and the long-term sustainability of your retirement portfolio could be in danger.

First Warning Indicator

> When you must sell at a loss any securities in your portfolio. It shows there's something wrong with your asset's allocation, diversification or withdrawal strategies. They might not be providing enough protection from the sequence of returns risk, or from the natural down periods all asset classes go through from time to time.

Second Warning Indicator

> When the percentage of the money you withdraw from your portfolio is higher than it should, or over 5% during the early years of a long retirement (30 years or more).

If during the performance review of your retirement plan you see any of these two indicators, take the time required to analyze what can be the problem, and what changes or adjustments you need to make to your strategy. Don't wait another year to do this.

Rebalance your Portfolio

Something you will need to do every year is to review how your portfolio's allocation is at that time, compared to the one established in your retirement plan, and perform any rebalancing that might be necessary. Multiple studies have shown that yearly rebalancing your portfolio, produces better results than doing it more frequently because of transaction costs and the tax impact.

Taking the Plunge

Once you have done your homework, defined the fundamental elements of your retirement plan and hopefully even tested them, go ahead and take the plunge.

Remember that given the number of variables involved in any retirement plan, and because we cannot estimate the behavior of a good amount of them with accuracy, it's impossible to create the perfect retirement plan. Don't fall victim of analysis paralysis.

If you made realistic assumptions, planned and took measures to manage even some possible but unexpected events and circumstances, the odds will be in your favor, and you will increase the likelihood of having a happy and enjoyable retirement.

Hopefully, this book leaves you with a clearer idea of all the aspects you need to take into consideration, how many of those aspects are interconnected, and how to create a realistic, practical, and useful retirement plan.

At the end of the book, you will find a list of resources and tools you can use to learn more about those aspects you may want to analyze in more detail.

I also included a retirement plan review guide, that can help you approach the preparation of your plan at your own pace, but in an orderly and systematic way. If you would like to print it or make some changes, you can download an MS Word file or a Google Docs version on my website at: moneyconsiderations.com/tools/

Good luck and happy retirement!

HOW TO PLAN FOR RETIREMENT (REVIEW GUIDE)

I. Factors Involved in a Successful Retirement

Your Professional Situation

- Does the company or organization you work for offers a retirement pension plan? ____
- If so, at what age can you participate? ____
- Is there any circumstance related to your job, that might influence the timing of your decision to retire (a project, restructuring, merger, acquisition, relocation, etc.)? ____
- Based on that circumstance, when would you like to retire? ___/___/___

Your Personal and Family Situations

In relation with your spouse/partner:

- Have you two discussed the issue? ____

- Considering your spouse or partner's situation, when would you like to retire? ___/___/___

About your children:

- Considering your children's situation, when would you like to retire? ___/___/___

In relation to your parents:

- Does their health or financial situation have any influence on you retiring? ____
- Considering your parents' situation, when would you like to retire? ___/___/___

II. Key Questions to Answer

- What do you want to do during retirement?
  ____
- Where do you want to spend your retirement?
  ____
- Do you have a few options you would like to consider? Yes ____ No ____
- How do they rate and compare to each other?

Characteristic	Option 1	Option 2	Option 3
Cost of Living			
Estate & Local Taxes			
Health Care Services			
Long-Term Care			
Airports			
Economy			
Crime			
Weather			
Total Points			

Note.- To evaluate each city/town, give it a rating from 0 to 10 for each characteristic, and add all the points you gave to each place to compare their total valuation.

The Healthcare Issue

If you retire before you are 65 years old, which options do you have available to cover your health care needs:

- COBRA ____
- Individual Insurance ____
- Health Savings Accounts ____
- Short-Term Insurance ____
- Direct Primary Care ____
- Faith-Based Healthcare ____

If you retire being 65 years or older, your health care will be provided within the framework of Medicare.

Things you should remember about Medicare:

- You should sign up for Medicare Part A when you turn 65.
- If you are still working, it will become secondary to your employer group coverage.
- You should enroll in Part D within six months surrounding when you become eligible for Medicare.
- You can sign up for Medicare Parts B and C at age 65 or when you come off your employer group coverage.
- Don't forget about the out-of-pocket costs you will have to cover.

III. The Financial Factor

Key factors you need to estimate:

- Your life expectancy: __ years
- The expected average annual rate of inflation: __ %
- Expected avg. annual return on your investments: __ %
- Estimated effective tax rate during retirement: __ %

Determine how much money you will need to retire

- Estimated income required at retirement: $__________
- Estimated future expenses at retirement: $__________
- Estimated fixed income at retirement: $__________

Difference between estimated fixed income and:

- Estimated income required at retirement: $__________

- Estimated future expenses at retirement: $__________
- Estimated savings required to finance your retirement $__________

Possible strategies to reduce the time required to accumulate the savings required for retirement or to try to reduce the amount of savings needed.

- Reduce expenses ____
- Increase savings ____
- Use the equity in your house: ____

Downsizing ____
Renting ____
Getting a reverse mortgage ____

- Getting an annuity ____
- Postponing retirement ____

How are you going to invest your retirement savings?

Determine what asset allocation strategy you will follow.

A) Keeping your age in bonds ____
B) Investing in balanced Funds or ETFs ____
C) Investing in target-date Funds ____
D) Based on your ability to handle losses ____
E) Based on your capacity to handle losses ____
F) The bucket strategy. ____

Determine:
How many buckets you will have ____
With what type of investment instruments ____
What percentage of your savings in each one ____

G) Using the 7Twelve™ System ____
H) Using the Level3 Strategy ____

Which withdrawal strategy you will use?

How are you going to determine your initial withdrawal?

- A dollar amount $________
- A % of your retirement savings ____.
- What percentage? ____%

What strategy will you follow to adjust the subsequent yearly withdrawals?

- A simple, direct adjustment based on inflation ____
- A dynamic strategy using a ceiling and a floor ____
- The feel free withdrawal strategy ____
- The investments earnings withdrawal strategy ____

Required Minimum Distributions (RMDs)

- Year in which you will have to take your first RMD? ____
- Deadline to take your first RMD __/__/__

Your taxes during retirement

- Is your assets location optimized to reduce your taxes? ____
- Do your investment portfolio and the investment instruments within it have a low turnover ratio? ____
- Do you know what the tax treatment of Social Security benefits is in the state where you are planning to retire? ____

Don't forget to file and pay estimated quarterly taxes once retired.

Planning for the unexpected

Have you evaluated the feasibility and convenience to get (or keep) some of the following types of insurance?

- Whole life insurance ____
- Long-term disability insurance ____
- Property Insurance ____
- An umbrella policy ____
- Long-term care insurance ____

Do you have all the documents you might need, so that someone you trust can make financial and healthcare decisions on your behalf, in case you become temporarily or permanently disabled? Or to make sure that if you pass away your assets pass to the people or entities you want?

- Durable Power of Attorney (or Financial Power of Attorney) ____
- Power of Attorney for Healthcare (or Health Care Proxy) ____
- Living Will (or Advance Directive) ____

III. Pre-tests and Tracking of Your Retirement Plan

Key issues to test before you retire

- If you are moving, have you spent enough time in the place where you plan to retire to make sure it will work for you? ____

- Have you tested that you can cover your expenses within your estimated Budget? ____
- Have you tried spending a reasonable amount of time doing what you plan to do during your retirement? ____

Track the performance of your Retirement Plan

Review your plan every quarter or at least twice a year, or every time your health, finances or lifestyle suffer an essential change.

If necessary, rebalance your retirement portfolio once a year.

Key factors you need to review:

- What was the annual return of your retirement portfolio last year, and how does it compare with the return you estimated in your plan?
- What was the annual inflation rate?
- Have your expenses been in line with the amounts you had estimated? Was any deviation temporal or a lasting trend?
- How does your effective yearly withdrawal compare with your estimated withdrawal? What caused the difference?

Review in detail all your financial estimates, if any of the below happens:

1. You need to sell at a loss any securities in your portfolio.
2. The money you withdraw for any year represents 5% or more of your total portfolio.

RESOURCES

Books

Barry, Patricia. *Medicare For Dummies (For Dummies (Business & Personal Finance)*. For Dummies, 2017.

Bernstein, William J. *The Intelligent Asset Allocator: How to Build Your Portfolio to Maximize Returns and Minimize Risk.* McGraw-Hill Education, 2017.

Bogle, John C. *The Little Book of Common Sense Investing: The Only Way to Guarantee Your Fair Share of Stock Market Returns.* Wiley, 2017.

Carlson, Robert C. *The New Rules of Retirement: Strategies for a Secure Future.* Wiley, 2016.

Hebeler, Henry K. *Getting Started in A Financially Secure Retirement: Pre- and Post-Retirement Planning in a Time of Great Uncertainty*. John Wiley and Sons, 2007.

Israelsen, Craig L. *7 Twelve: A Diversified Investment Portfolio with a Plan*. John Wiley and Sons, 2010.

Jason, Julie. *The AARP Retirement Survival Guide: How to Make Smart Financial Decisions in Good Times and Bad.* Sterling, 2009.

Kirkpatrick, Darrow. *Can I Retire Yet?: How to Make the Biggest Financial Decision of the Rest of Your Life.* StructureByDesign, 2016.

Larsen, Bruce. *A Concise Guide to Taxes in Retirement.* Bruce Larsen, 2016.

Moeller, Philip. *Get What's Yours for Medicare: Maximize Your Coverage, Minimize Your Costs.* Simon & Schuster, 2016.

Piper, Mike. *Can I Retire?: How Much Money You Need to Retire and How to Manage Your Retirement Savings, Explained in 100 Pages or Less.* Simple Subjects, LLC, 2016.

Piper, Mike. *Social Security Made Simple: Social Security Retirement Benefits and Related Planning Topics Explained in 100 Pages or Less.* Simple Subjects, LLC, 2017.

Quinn, Jane Bryant. *How to Make Your Money Last: The Indispensable Retirement Guide.* Simon & Schuster, 2016.

Risley, Jean. *How to Decide What to Do Next When You're Retired: Put Your Time and Energy Where Your Values Are.* Risley Resources, 2016.

Sterk, Mary. *Ready to Pull the Retirement Trigger?: Your Strategic Guide to Retire With Confidence.* Morgan James Publishing, 2017.

Steuer, Tony. *Insurance Made Easy: A Comprehensive Roadmap to the Coverage You Need.* Life Insurance Sage Press, 2017.

Wacasey, Kevin. *The Guide to Buying Health Insurance, and Health Care.* CreateSpace, 2016.

Blogs/Websites

General information about retirement issues:

- Bob Carlson's Retirement Watch - retirementwatch.com
- The Retirement Manifesto - theretirementmanifesto.com
- Can I Retire Yet? - caniretireyet.com
- Kiplinger - kiplinger.com/fronts/channels/retirement/index.html
- The Official U.S. Government site for Medicare - medicare.gov

Retirement Calculators

- New Retirement - newretirement.com
- MaxiFi - maxifiplanner.com
- ESPlanner - esplanner.com
- Fidelity Retirement Income Planner - fidelity.com/calculators-tools/planning-guidance-center
- OnTrajectory - ontrajectory.com
- Retire Fit - arnexa.com/retirefit.html
- Real World Retirement Software - toolsformoney.com/retirement_software.htm
- The Flexible Retirement Planner - flexibleretirementplanner.com/wp/
- SimplePlanning.com - Simpleplanning.com

Networks of Fee-only Financial Planners

- The Garrett Planning Network - GarrettPlanningNetwork.com

- The National Association of Personal Financial Advisors - NAPFA.org
- The Financial Planning Association - plannersearch.org

Online Tools

- City-Data.com - city-data.com
- BestPlaces - bestplaces.net
- Social Security Benefit Calculators:
- Social Security Quick Calculator - ssa.gov/OACT/quickcalc/
- Social Security Retirement Benefits Estimator - ssa.gov/benefits/retirement/estimator.html
- New York Times Rent vs buying Calculator - nytimes.com/interactive/2014/upshot/buy-rent-calculator.html
- Bankrate Asset Allocation Calculator - bankrate.com/calculators/retirement/asset-allocation.aspx
- Annual Returns on Stock, T.Bonds and T.Bills:1928-Current: stern.nyu.edu/~adamodar/pc/datasets/histretSP.xls
- Price of Immediate Annuities: immediateannuities.com

THANK YOU

Thanks for reading this book. I hope you found it useful and enjoyed reading it.

I would appreciate if you could please leave a review on Amazon. Even a line or two would help me bring this book to the attention of potential readers. Thank you very much.

This book is the second in the series "Take Control of Your Finances." Every book in the series aims to provide practical information presented in a plain-spoken way about how to improve and better manage different aspects of your finances.

ABOUT THE AUTHOR

H. Dominguez (HD) has been a business consultant for more than twenty years, working with a broad range of businesses and organizations in multiple industries. Before starting his consulting practice, he worked as a corporate lawyer in the petrochemical industry. He has always been keenly interested in personal finance and keeps the blog Money Considerations. HD lives in Connecticut.

Also by H. Dominguez:

How to Control Your Money: Reduce Your Debt and Increase Your Savings.

You can connect with HD on:

Website: www.moneyconsiderations.com

Email: hd@moneyconsiderations.com

facebook.com/MoneyConsiderations

twitter.com/HDominguezMC

NOTES

1. https://www.myirionline.org/docs/default-source/research/iri_babyboomers_whitepaper_2018_final.pdf
2. https://www.bls.gov/cex/2017/combined/age.pdf
3. https://www.planadviser.com/mere-16-fortune-500-companies-offer-db-plan/
4. https://www.kiplinger.com/slideshow/retirement/T051-S001-37-states-that-don-t-tax-social-security-benefits/index.html
5. https://fredblog.stlouisfed.org/2017/07/healthy-inflation/
6. https://www.fidelity.com/viewpoints/retirement/protect-your-retirement-income
7. Genworth 2017 Cost of Care Survey
8. http://www.usinflationcalculator.com/inflation/historical-inflation-rates/
9. http://pages.stern.nyu.edu/~adamodar
10. https://nfcc.org/wp-content/uploads/2018/04/NFCC_BECU_2018-FLS_datasheet-with-key-findings_031318-002.pdf
11. https://www.bls.gov/cex/2017/combined/age.pdf
12. https://www.bls.gov/cex/2017/combined/age.pdf

13. https://www.ssa.gov/news/press/factsheets/basicfact-alt.pdf
14. http://www.nber.org/papers/w24226?mod=article_inline
15. https://www.bls.gov/cex/2017/combined/age.pdf
16. https://www.marketwatch.com/story/the-dow-may-already-be-in-a-bear-market-heres-how-long-it-could-last-2018-03-27
17. http://pages.stern.nyu.edu/~adamodar

INDEX

Made in the USA
Middletown, DE
21 February 2019